CULTURES OF THE WORLD

CUBA

SEAN SHEEHAN

MARSHALL CAVENDISH
New York • London • Sydney

Reference edition published 1995 by
Marshall Cavendish Corporation
2415 Jerusalem Avenue
P.O. Box 587
North Bellmore
New York 11710

© Times Editions Pte Ltd 1995

Originated and designed by
Times Books International, an imprint of
Times Editions Pte Ltd

Printed in Singapore

Library of Congress Cataloging-in-Publication Data:
Sheehan, Sean.
   Cuba / Sean Sheehan
      p. cm.—(Cultures Of The World)
   Includes bibliographical references (p.   ) and index.
   ISBN 1-85435-691-7 :
   1. Cuba—Juvenile literature. [1. Cuba.]
I. Title. II. Series.
F1758.5.S54 1994
972.91—dc20   94–22574
                   CIP
                    AC

Cultures of the World

Editorial Director	Shirley Hew
Managing Editor	Shova Loh
Editors	Elizabeth Berg
	Jacquiline King
	Dinah Lee
	Azra Moiz
	Sue Sismondo
Picture Editor	Susan Jane Manuel
Production	Anthony Chua
Design	Tuck Loong
	Ronn Yeo
	Felicia Wong
	Loo Chuan Ming
Illustrators	Anuar
	Chow Kok Keong
	William Sim
MCC Editorial Director	Evelyn M. Fazio
MCC Production Manager	Janet Castiglioni

INTRODUCTION

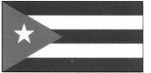

CUBA IS A DYNAMIC COUNTRY that presents a challenging face to the rest of the world. Its colonial history has a lot in common with other Caribbean islands, but after Fidel Castro came to power in 1959 virtually all aspects of life underwent radical change and experimentation. People's working lives, leisure activities, art, religion, and their perceptions of each other and what it means to be Cuban were all transformed by a cultural and political revolution.

Cuba is now facing crucial choices as an economic crisis, mainly the result of the loss of aid from Russia, threatens to tear apart its social fabric. The United States, home to the largest community of expatriate Cubans, continues to play a significant role in Cuba's unfolding drama. This book portrays the life and times of Cuba, its cultural richness and excitement as well as its economic and social ills. The country's future now hangs in the balance, and the following pages capture this critical period in Cuba's development.

CONTENTS

Cuban teens with street graffiti.

CONTENTS

A Cuban flag and a portrait of Fidel Castro share the space on a shop wall with various notices.

GEOGRAPHY

CUBA, THE WORLD'S SEVENTH LARGEST ISLAND, is the largest of the Caribbean Islands, an archipelago bordered to the south by South America and to the west by Central America. The islands are the visible summit of a submerged mountain range that once joined North and South America. Cuba, 750 miles long and ranging in width from 25 to 120 miles, lies 90 miles south of Florida and 90 miles east of Mexico. It is about the same size as the state of Pennsylvania.

TOPOGRAPHY

The island of Cuba itself makes up just under 95% of the national territory; there is also the Isle of Youth near the southwestern coast and some 1,600 islets, most of them uninhabited.

MOUNTAINS The island of Cuba is mostly made up of flatlands and rolling plains, but mountains in the western and eastern extremities and in central Cuba cover almost a quarter of the total land mass.

The largest mountain range, the Sierra Maestra, is over a hundred miles long and contains the highest peak at Pico Turquino (6,540 feet). Another striking feature of the Sierra Maestra is Gran Piedra (Huge Rock), characterized by a sheer face that stretches to its summit at 4,024 feet.

The central mountain range includes the Sierra de Trinidad, where summits rarely exceed 3,500 feet and roads and railway lines are able to cross the mountains to link the southern shore with the northern coastline.

The Sierra de los Organos in the west is the lowest of the three main ranges, never exceeding 2,000 feet and containing a number of limestone caves.

Opposite: **Dramatic landscape of the Viñales Valley in a minor range in west Cuba, the Sierra del Rosario, just east of the Sierra de los Organos. Once covered with forests, much of the land has been cleared for farming and only a few wooded areas remain.**

Above: **The peak of Gran Piedra in the Sierra Maestra.**

7

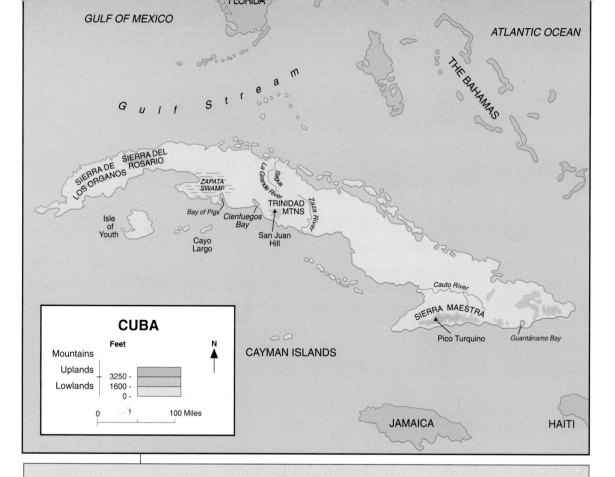

A STUDY IN CONTRAST: TWO CUBAN ISLANDS

The Isle of Youth, Cuba's largest offshore island with a total area of 1,160 square miles, is situated 60 miles south of the mainland. Out of its population of about 100,000 there are over 15,000 young foreign students, mainly from Africa. Therefore, the island's name was changed from Isle of Pines to Isle of Youth in 1978. In the past, the physical isolation of the island made it a suitable site for incarcerating political prisoners, and in 1931 President Gerardo Machado ordered the construction of a maximum security prison, based on the plans for a similar prison in Joliet, Illinois. Fidel Castro is the Isle of Youth's most famous former prisoner, and the prison is a prime tourist attraction. Only the north side of the island is developed, while most of the southern side is undeveloped woodland and swampland, mostly inhabited by fishermen and their families.

Another of the few inhabited Cuban islands is Cayo Largo. It is 15 miles long and up to five miles wide and is situated 75 miles east of the Isle of Youth, some 50 miles south of the mainland. Geographically, it is little more than a strip of sand in the ocean and its entire southern coast is one long beach. As such, it has been entirely given over to tourism, and the only Cubans allowed on the island are those working in the tourist industry. The currency used on Cayo Largo is the American dollar, and because the majority of visitors tend to be affluent Europeans seeking a sun-and-beach vacation, Cayo Largo's resorts earn valuable foreign currency.

CLIMATE

The climate is temperate and semitropical. The moderating influence is due to trade winds that blow westward across the island. Cuba's dry season lasts from November to April and the wet season from May through October. The average minimum temperature is 70°F and the average maximum is 81°F. Temperatures occasionally exceed 100°F in the summer, and during the winter, freezing temperatures are sometimes recorded in the high mountain areas.

Rainfall is generally moderate with three-quarters of the annual precipitation occurring during the wet season. While some years are characterized by drought, others receive very heavy rainfall. The uneven nature of the rainfall helps to explain why central Cuba has some fairly dry lowlands where cacti are common, while in the eastern part of the island tropical rainforest can also be found.

Cuba lies in the track of fierce tropical hurricanes; during the wet season the island experiences on average one hurricane every two years. Winds of over 160 miles an hour in addition to 12 inches of rainfall in a period of 24 hours can cause extensive damage. In 1963, Hurricane Flora killed over 4,000 people and destroyed some 30,000 homes.

The semitropical Cuban climate supports year-round vegetation in all parts of the island.

WATERWAYS

Nearly 600 rivers in Cuba, mostly short and unnavigable, ensures that the land is well irrigated and suitable for agriculture. The two longest rivers are the Zaza, in central Cuba, and the Cauto, in eastern Cuba, north of the Sierra Maestra mountain range.

The most interesting lake in Cuba is the 26 square mile Laguna de Leche (Milky Lagoon) in central Cuba. Since a number of channels connect the lagoon with the sea, tidal movements disturb the calcium carbonate deposits that form the floor of the lagoon and give rise to its milky appearance.

Crocodiles and alligators live along the coastal marshes and within the labyrinth of small rivers. There are large enclosed zones where thousands of these animals are farmed for their meat and their hides.

Cuba boasts 200 natural ports, of which about 20 function commercially as points for the export of products like sugar.

Right: **The smallest amphibian in the world, the Banana Frog, is found in Cuba.**

Opposite: **The Cuban Trogon.**

FLORA AND FAUNA

The smallest amphibian in the world, the Banana Frog, and the tiniest mammal in the world, the Almiqui, are both found in Cuba. The Almiqui is a shrew-like creature with long claws for catching the insects it feeds on. The smallest scorpion in the world can also be encountered in Cuba—if your eyes are sharp enough to spot the female of the species, which is less than a tenth of an inch long. Another minuscule creature is the *Polymita* genus of snail, only found in the northeast of Cuba and believed by the ancient Afro-Cubans to have magical powers. None of the 14 species of snakes inhabiting the island are poisonous, although one of them, the boa, kills by suffocating its prey by constriction and can grow to 13 feet in length.

Nearly 400 species of birds have been recorded on the island, including the Bee Hummingbird, the smallest in the world. Because it measures only half an inch, including the bill and tail, it is often confused with an insect. Equally distinctive, though for a different reason, is the Sijus bird, which is capable of turning its head a full 360 degrees. One of the most eye-catching of the island's birds is the Cuban Trogon, a member of the *Trogonidae* family that is made up of 35 species that inhabit the tropical forests of the Americas, Africa, and Asia. It is about the size of a small crow and is largely metallic green with bright patches of the three colors that make up the country's flag—black, red, and white—thus helping to confirm its status as Cuba's national bird.

Butterflies and moths contribute a dimension of their own to the kaleidoscope of color that characterizes the flora and fauna of Cuba. There are more than 180 species of butterflies and nearly 30 of these are found only on the island. Their colorful displays can be imagined when they bear names like Orange Sulphur, Mosaic, and Cuban Buff Zebra.

ANUAR

FLOWERS AND TREES GALORE

Some 20% of Cuba's land is covered by forests and woods so not surprisingly there is a tremendous assortment of trees and flowers. Especially large are the flame trees (see below) and the African tulip trees that provide shade during the heat of the day and advertise their presence by grand lily-like blooms. The frangipani, whose flowers are used for garlands, is common. There are over 8,000 floral varieties, ranging from the rare *flor San Pedro* orchid to the ubiquitous hibiscus and African golden trumpet. The climate encourages a colorful mixture of flowers to flourish around buildings, and a typically eye-catching home in the countryside may have pink or white congea climbing the walls and bougainvilleas of magenta, mauve, red, and orange crowding the path to the door.

The value of Cuban wood was appreciated by the Spanish who used it to build their fleet of ships transporting treasure across the Atlantic. Today there is commercial value in the sale of mahogany, ebony, oak, and teak. The bark of mahogany is also used to treat ailments, including rheumatism and pneumonia. Cuba has more than 60 species of palm trees including the stately *palma real* (royal palm), Cuba's national tree that grows to over 75 feet tall. The versatile tamarind tree found lining roads bears fruit pods used as a flavoring, a preservative, and a medicine, besides being a commercially valuable timber. Along the coastline grow almond, mangrove, and wild fig trees. Cuba's rarest tree is the cork palm, found only in the western half of the island and classified as a living fossil because it goes back 100,000,000 years to the Cretaceous Period.

LIFE IN THE WATER

With some 900 different species of fish to be found around Cuba, it is not surprising that they attract humans for a variety of reasons. The American writer Ernest Hemingway, who lived in Cuba for a number of years, was an enthusiast of game fishing. The chance to catch a marlin, probably the fastest-swimming fish in the world, still draws tourists. Various prestigious international fishing tournaments are held, including the Hemingway Marlin Fishing Tournament begun by the writer in 1950. Many local competitions engage the talents of Cubans.

Above: **The distinctively marked clown fish is found in Cuban waters.**

Opposite: **The Flame Tree ablaze with color.**

The warm waters of the Atlantic Ocean, the Gulf of Mexico, and the Caribbean Sea are home to a myriad collection of coral reefs and tropical fish with endearing names: clown fish, queen angelfish, tangs, porgies, pez perro, and gorgonia. On the surface, turtles swim placidly and share the water with dolphins and porpoises, while above them flying fish open their pectoral fins and scull the water with their tails to gain momentum. Underwater, the colorful fish life can be appreciated with little more equipment than a pair of goggles. One acknowledgment of the country's rich underwater life is the fact that the World Underwater Film Festival has been held in Cuba.

Some of the fish to be found in Cuban waters are best kept at a safe distance. These include moray eels, up to five feet long with sharp teeth that discourage divers from getting too close. Equally voracious predators are the barracudas, whose fang-like teeth have been used against bathers and divers.

13

Some 70% of nonsugar manufacturing activity is centered around Havana, making it easily the busiest city on the island. Like all industrial cities, it suffers from air pollution.

HAVANA

Three out of four Cubans live in urban areas. The largest city is Havana, the capital of Cuba in the northeast of the main island, with a population of over two million. The total population of the island is approaching 11 million, reflecting the fact that Havana is the largest industrial center on the island.

One of the most built-up areas in the capital is Habana Vieja (Old Havana), the old colonial city situated on the shores of Havana Bay. The old part of Havana contains a number of buildings of outstanding architectural interest that date back to the period of Spanish colonization. Old Havana has been listed by UNESCO (United Nations Educational, Scientific, and Cultural Organization) as a "world heritage city" and is helping to restore many of these buildings. In response to the growing urban population, new housing programs have developed smaller townships in the suburbs.

OTHER CITIES

The largest city after Havana is Santiago de Cuba, which is situated on the southeastern end of the island, scenically located overlooking a bay and nestled by the foothills of the Sierra Maestra mountains. Around 400,000 people live there, many of whom are Cubans working at the United States naval base at Guantánamo Bay less than 100 miles away. Santiago de Cuba has an international airport and the country's second busiest port. Other sources of employment are provided by numerous factories near the city, an oil refinery, and power stations. It is a very cosmopolitan city, due partly to the mix of African and Spanish heritages.

One astonishing feature of Havana—considering its size and its social and political status as the country's capital city—is the relative absence of traffic noise. A gasoline shortage has drastically reduced the amount of traffic.

Santiago de Cuba, founded by the Spanish as the country's capital, is today known as the "capital of the Revolution" because of its historical association with the overthrow of Fulgencio Batista's dictatorship (see page 25). It was here in 1953 that a small group of rebels launched a surprise attack on the Moncada Barracks, an event regarded as a pivotal moment in Cuba's modern history.

The next most important city is Camagüey, situated in the center of Camagüey province between Havana and Santiago de Cuba. This province is one of Cuba's most prosperous regions, mainly due to its cattle and tobacco, and Camagüey is one of the island's oldest industrial cities. Cubans identify the city with the production of *tinajones* ("tin-a-HON-es"), clay urns 10 feet wide and five feet tall placed outside houses, often buried up to half their height in the ground, for the storage of cool water. Although they are no longer used for this purpose, their presence outside buildings in Camugüey is a characteristic sight.

HISTORY

CUBA'S STRATEGIC LOCATION in the Caribbean at the mouth of the Gulf of Mexico has played an important part in the island's history. The Spanish used Cuba's natural harbors as ports for ships plying between the New World and Spain. In the 20th century, Cuba's proximity to the United States made its internal politics and foreign relations with Communist countries particularly significant.

Throughout Cuba's history, a pattern of tensions between major players has been repeated: conquering Spanish colonialists and early inhabitants, Spanish imperial government and a racially mixed Cuban population, landowners and peasants, the United States and Cuba.

EARLY INHABITANTS

Cuba's earliest known inhabitants were the Ciboney and Guanahatabey, who lived in the western half of the island. The more numerous Taíno arrived much later, around A.D. 1200. Evidence of cave-dwelling tribes dates back to 3500 B.C., and includes pictographs of magical signs and sky charts, and caves used for ritual purposes.

The Taíno were closely related to the Arawaks of South America and the two groups are often spoken of as one people. It is very likely that these early settlers on Cuba were descendants of agriculturalists who had migrated north from the Amazon Basin of South America.

Opposite: **The past has left behind a heritage of old buildings, such as this one with a typical Spanish colonial facade in Old Havana.**

Below: **The peasant dwelling called a** *bohío*. **Taíno Indians lived in huts like these, which are still seen in the rural and mountain areas of Cuba. The roof thatch is made of palm leaves or grasses and the walls are usually of palm wood.**

CONQUERING THE TAÍNO

The Taíno lived in village communities varying in size from a few families to a few thousand people. Each community had a leader. They raised crops like potatoes and manioc, grew vegetables like yam, and caught fish and birds to eat. They wove cotton, cultivated the tobacco plant, and produced their own stone tools. Little is known about their religious beliefs, but idols were carved out of stone, wood, and clay.

The peaceful culture of the Taíno was ill-suited to meet the challenge of Spanish invaders who first landed on the island with Christopher Columbus on October 27, 1492. In later years more Spanish arrived and they had little trouble subduing the Indians. The Taíno were forced into slavery; those who resisted were killed. A missionary who accompanied the Spanish described how the Spanish repaid the hospitality of the Taíno who fed them by raping women and killing entire village populations. Children starved to death when parents were rounded up to work in mines.

The actual settlement of Cuba by Spain began in 1511. By then, other Caribbean islands had been settled. The leader of one Haitian community, Chief Hatuey, fled to Cuba with 400 survivors and tried to convince the Cuban Taíno to resist the invaders, but they mistrusted him. Hatuey went into hiding, joined by some Taíno, and when the Spanish arrived, he led his followers in guerrilla warfare against the Spanish. But their arrows were no match for horses and gunpowder, and their ambushes only delayed the inevitable. Hatuey was captured and, when he refused to reveal the location of his people, burned at the stake. Within a very short time the Taíno faced extinction. They died fighting the invaders or from disease and overwork in mines and on plantations controlled by the Spanish.

SPANISH RULE

In 1511, Diego Velázquez de Cuéllar arrived to establish a permanent settlement at Baracoa. The Spanish came to Cuba looking for gold. Rivers were panned and mines dug by the Taíno, and when more labor was needed slaves from Africa were shipped to the island. When Cuba's yield of gold was found to be poor, the Spanish turned elsewhere. In 1519, a large expedition that included some 3,000 Indians left Cuba under the command of Hernán Cortés, lured to the Aztec empire in Mexico by tales of unlimited riches. The African slaves were left on the island with the remaining Taíno Indians, to work on plantations in a system known as *encomienda*—work in return for "protection" and conversion to Catholicism.

The remainder of the 16th century witnessed the decline and final elimination of the Taíno population. Black slaves became more important on plantations, although the development of Cuba's real wealth—sugar and tobacco—was slow. More and more Spanish ships stopped at Cuba in transatlantic crossings, laden with plunder from Mexico and Central and South America. The harbor at Havana was developed, and toward the end of the 16th century Morro Castle was built at the harbor entrance, signifying Cuba's newfound importance.

Above: **Havana's Morro Castle, a fort against piracy, was built by the Spanish between 1589 and 1630. The lighthouse at the entrance was added in 1844.**

Opposite: **Taíno Indians panning and mining for gold under the watchful eyes of the Spanish.**

Above: **A few of Cuba's remaining gauchos or cowboys. Cuba's central plains were ideal pastures for cattle ranching. By the end of the 18th century, however, much grazing land was given over to the cultivation of the more profitable sugarcane.**

CUBA BECOMES IMPORTANT It was well into the 18th century before the Spanish settlement in Cuba showed commercial success. Ships brought thousands of new slaves as sugar and tobacco became more profitable due to increased European demand and the opening of trade with the Spanish colonies and North America. Havana emerged as the obvious capital of the island as the harbor developed its own shipbuilding industry to complement its role as a major naval base.

Havana became sufficiently important to gain the attention of the British, who occupied the harbor and town in 1762 and stayed there for nearly a year before the Spanish regained control. By 1774 a census showed that the population had reached over 170,000, consisting of 44,000 blacks, 96,000 whites, and 31,000 people of mixed parentage.

During the decades that followed, the population was swelled by thousands of French colonists who fled neighboring Haiti seeking refuge from an uprising of Haitians. In 1801, Haiti invaded the island of Hispaniola and the Spanish colonists who had controlled part of the island also fled to Cuba. Two years later, when Louisiana was sold to the United States by France, more European colonials came to an increasingly prosperous Cuba. By the first decade of the 19th century, Cuba was economically self-sufficient and no longer depended on cash subsidies from Spain.

REVOLT AGAINST SPAIN

Long before the American slave trade ended in 1865 (slavery in Cuba was abolished in 1886) the population of Cuba was further mixed by the arrival of indentured Chinese laborers. The island's economy was booming, due chiefly to the sugar industry, and Cuba needed an alternative source of labor because of growing incidents of slave uprisings. A focus of discontent at the time was the perception by native-born Cubans known as *criollos* ("kree-OH-yohs," or Creoles) that they were being discriminated against in favor of the *peninsulares* ("pay-nin-SOO-lah-rehs," or Spanish-born Cubans). The government in Spain handed power and privileges to their own kind, the *peninsulares.*

By the mid-19th century, *peninsulares* and *criollos* clashed frequently in the pursuit of opposite aims. The *peninsulares* were mainly military personnel, government representatives, landowners, and slave-owners who preferred Spanish rule. The *criollos* included teachers, professionals, and writers, some of whom owned slaves. The *criollos* were divided, one group wanting independence from Spain but maintaining slavery, the other freedom for everyone in Cuba.

Meanwhile, the United States was becoming increasingly interested in Cuba's economy and politics. Its offers to buy the island from Spain were officially rejected while attracting support within the business community on the island. Among the rebels watched closely by Cuba's powerful northern neighbor were Carlos Manuel de Céspedes, Antonio Maceo y Grajales, and the best-loved and remembered of Cuban patriots, José Martí.

The Cuban rebel leader Antonio Maceo was known as the Bronze Titan.

"CUBA LIBRE!" (FREE CUBA)

The first major revolt, known as the Ten Years' War because it lasted from 1868 to 1878, actually started with *El Grito de Yara* ("the cry of Yara"). Yara was the town near the plantation of Carlos Manuel de Céspedes, a wealthy lawyer. He and 37 other landowners freed their slaves and proclaimed (the "cry") the independence of Cuba from Spain. Ambushed by Spanish troops toward the end of the war, Manuel killed himself to escape capture.

The uneasy peace concluded in 1878 did not solve the central issue of Cuba's status. Spain was willing to liberalize its colonial rule, but calls for independence or incorporation into the United States were not answered. The inconclusive Ten Years' War left 50,000 Cubans and 208,000 Spanish dead.

Antonio Maceo, known to Cubans as the Bronze Titan, joined the rebels toward the end of the war. He contributed greatly to the guerrilla tactics of the rebels. When not ambushing the Spanish, he read widely and organized the rebels' living quarters, including hospitals and food stores, with the help of his mother and wife. After the Ten Years' War, he left for Jamaica with his family, continuing the revolutionary struggle from abroad. There he met José Martí (pictured above), whom many call the Apostle of Freedom.

A war of independence erupted again in 1895, with both sides showing a grim determination to resolve the conflict through violence. The rebels were led by José Martí, whose rallying call was *"Cuba Libre."* Within three years Spain controlled only the coastal towns.

Martí was convinced of the need for Cuba to develop as an independent country. When only 16 he was sentenced to hard labor in a stone quarry, imprisoned on the Isle of Pines, then banished to Spain because of his political opinions. In Spain he graduated with a law degree in 1874 and his revolutionary fervor expressed itself in poetry and prose. Banned from Cuba, Marti traveled to the United States where he campaigned relentlessly for an independent Cuba. He established the Cuban Revolutionary Party in New York and sought to enlist the aid of the United States government, but it was not prepared to help him officially. In 1895, he organized an armed force that landed in Cuba. Thousands of Cubans died in the rebellion that followed, including José Martí, who was killed during an encounter with troops loyal to the Spanish government.

The best loved leader of the Cuban revolution died when he was only 42. Many statues have been erected in his memory. Generally less well known is the fact that he was the grandfather of movie star César Romero, and that he wrote the verses of the famous song *Guantanamera.*

UNITED STATES RULE

At first, the United States remained officially neutral during the tumultuous events in Cuba, though secretly negotiating with Spain to purchase the island. American business companies, by then the dominant investors in Cuba's sugar industry, called for American intervention in Cuba to protect their interests. Then in 1898, an event occurred that caused the United States to enter the war.

The battleship *U.S.S. Maine* was sent to Havana with the ostensible mission of helping to evacuate American citizens endangered by the fighting between Cuban revolutionaries and loyalist forces. When the ship exploded in the harbor, under circumstances that have never been fully explained, the United States blamed Spain and declared war on the country. This was the start of the Spanish-American War.

With American troops as well as nationalist rebels fighting against the loyalist troops, the war came to an end in August 1898. In December 1898, under the Treaty of Paris, Spain relinquished its claim to the island. An American military government was set up to govern the island.

For three years following the Treaty of Paris, Cuba was governed by the U.S. Army General Leonard Wood. The army was mainly engaged in public works programs, like the building of schools and roads, in order to facilitate American economic and cultural development of the island.

Although the United States brought order to the war-torn island, many Cubans believed they had changed one undesirable master for another. There was also a sense of bitterness that, through one single incident, the revolutionaries had been denied the glory of winning a war that had lasted decades and cost so many Cuban lives.

Cuban physician Carlos Findlay, in 1881, first argued the view that the deadly yellow fever was carried by mosquitoes. U.S. army doctors investigated the claim, and in 1900 were able to confirm it. A mosquito control program led to the disease's subsequent eradication.

Images of Ernesto (Che) Guevara, Fidel Castro's close revolutionary partner, are everywhere in Cuba. The nickname *Che* is Argentinian for "Hey, man!" and Guevara loved using the word in his speeches. Devoted to revolutionary causes, he inspired Fidel Castro to a similar dedication that led Castro to support revolutions in other parts of Latin America.

SELF-RULE?

To satisfy Cuban nationalism, the United States administration helped draw up a new constitution in 1901 that granted Cuba a degree of self-rule in 1902. But Afro-Cubans were denied the vote, and the Platt Amendment (authored by Senator Orville Hitchcock Platt), which the United States insisted had to be part of the constitution, established the right of the United States to intervene in the island's affairs. The amendment also gave the United States the right to buy or lease land for naval bases. Accordingly, in 1903, a permanent lease on Guantánamo Bay was granted to the United States; the naval base is still in operation today.

CORRUPTION

From 1906 to 1910 American troops returned to the island because of frequent uprisings against government leaders more interested in accumulating power and personal wealth than in the people's welfare. During the 1920s a dramatic rise in the price of sugar brought prosperity, but because American companies owned most of the profitable concerns, most Cubans were denied the fruits of economic success.

When the Great Depression in the 1930s worsened the already bad conditions, the rule of President Gerardo Machado was seriously threatened. In 1933, he was deposed by an army coup, and in 1934 an army sergeant, Fulgencio Batista, emerged with American support as Cuba's dictator.

BATISTA'S DICTATORSHIP

Fulgencio Batista (1901–1973) ruled as commander in chief of the armed forces from 1934 to 1940, when he became president. The constitution allowed a president to serve only one term in office. In 1952, however, Batista staged a second coup and ruled as Cuba's dictator for six years before being deposed himself.

Batista's Cuba prospered due to his government's repression of trade unions. Foreign companies set up business in Cuba and exported their profits. Little money went into public works as large-scale corruption permeated every aspect of political life.

Havana became the playground of the wealthy with its profusion of casinos, bars, and brothels. The tourists who filled Havana's casinos were oblivious to the poverty underpinning the private wealth of a minority of politicians and their close supporters. In the rural areas especially, many families could barely feed themselves and it was common to see malnourished children.

CASTRO'S REVOLUTION

Above: **Fulgencio Batista.**

The young lawyer Fidel Castro had planned to contest the 1952 elections, but when these never took place he adopted more direct action. On July 26, 1953 he led a small group in an attack on Moncada Barracks in Santiago de Cuba. The rebellion failed and Castro was imprisoned.

After his release in 1955, Castro went to Mexico to plan a second attempt at overthrowing the Batista dictatorship. A close colleague at this stage was the famous Argentinian revolutionary, Che Guevara. In December 1956, Castro, Che Guevara, and 80 others landed in eastern Cuba. Most of the group were killed or captured, but 12 men hid in the Sierra Maestra.

Over the next two years an increasingly successful guerrilla campaign was conducted against the government. The initial group of 12 was joined by supporters who shared their vision of freedom. The rebels gained the support of ordinary Cubans, including housewives, students, and even professional groups.

Elections were organized for November 3, 1958. Batista's chosen supporter was elected president, but it meant little. Soon after, the army deserted Batista, who fled Cuba on January 1, 1959. The rebel army marched into Havana on January 8, and a new era in Cuba's history began.

"Condemn me. It does not matter. History will absolve me."

—Fidel Castro, at his trial after the failed attack on Moncada Barracks

A billboard shouts defiance at the United States: "We're not scared of you, Mr. Imperialist."

FRICTION WITH THE UNITED STATES

The downfall of Batista's repressive government was hailed as a triumphant victory both in Cuba and around the world. The corruption and inequality that characterized Batista's Cuba had long been known. Over the next couple of years, however, relations between Cuba and the United States deteriorated and by January 1961 diplomatic relations between the two countries were formally broken off.

The rupture was caused by Castro's determination to build a revolutionary new society based on socialism. The Cuban government closed down casinos, lowered rents by 50%, and put industries under state control. The principal losers were American companies or individuals who owned these enterprises and buildings. American-owned sugar estates and cattle ranches were taken over in 1959–1960, then oil refineries. It is estimated that $1 billion in U.S.-owned properties were expropriated by the Cuban government. As a result, the U.S. government imposed a trade embargo against Cuba in October 1960. All remaining U.S. assets were then seized by the Cuban government.

Cuban refugees poured into the United States after the downfall of the Batista government. They included officials of the Batista government and those involved in corruption and vice as well as ordinary Cuban citizens opposed to Castro. Many of the exiles formed an underground movement

Friction with the United States

The U.S. government claims that $5.8 billion is owed by Cuba as a result of expropriating U.S.-owned property after the 1958 revolution.

to plan the invasion of Cuba. In late 1959, sporadic firebomb attacks by some exiles, using American planes and ammunition, though not officially sanctioned by the United States, increased tension between the countries.

In February 1960, Cuba and the Soviet Union signed their first trade agreement. As Russian trade and assistance grew, the American government became increasingly concerned by Castro's leftist leanings. In 1961, the United States supported an attempt by Cuban exiles opposed to Castro to invade the island at the Bay of Pigs.

Fidel Castro's tank from the Bay of Pigs incident.

THE BAY OF PIGS INCIDENT

The aim of Operation Pluto, the secret name of the invasion planned by the exiles with help from the American CIA, was to train 1,500 Cuban exiles, arm them, and help them land on Cuba, where Cubans were expected to welcome their "liberators."

It started with the bombing of two Cuban airfields on April 15, 1961, which killed seven and wounded 44. The American planes used were marked with the Cuban military insignia, to give the illusion of a military uprising. Rumors of the landing alerted the Cuban authorities, who rounded up anti-government suspects, including foreign journalists and CIA agents.

The invasion force landed on April 17 in the Bay of Pigs at Playa Giron. Within 48 hours, the invaders were captured. The incident increased Castro's popularity, especially since he was seen in action, organizing troops at Playa Giron. About 120 men were killed in the confrontation, and nearly 1,200 captured. The leaders were returned to the United States in exchange for cash, and the rest in exchange for medicine and food.

The locations of Russian missile sites, U.S. air bases, and naval blockade at the height of the missile crisis.

THE CUBAN MISSILE CRISIS OF 1962

In 1962, the world came perilously close to a nuclear war. As Cuba became more isolated by the hostility of the United States, it increasingly turned to the Soviet Union for support. The Soviet Union responded to Cuba's request for military assistance to reduce the risk of another American-backed invasion like the abortive Bay of Pigs incident.

In the summer of 1962 spy planes gathered photographic evidence of Soviet missile installations in Cuba. The United States felt threatened because the missiles had a range of 1,000 miles and Soviet jet bombers, also in Cuba, were capable of carrying nuclear weapons. On October 24, 1962 President John F. Kennedy warned his country of the threat from a nuclear attack and demanded that the Soviet Union dismantle the sites. He made it clear that not dismantling the missile sites would be viewed as a hostile act justifying nuclear retaliation by the United States.

The United States put a naval blockade around Cuba to halt the further shipment of arms. On October 26, 1962 Soviet premier Nikita Khrushchev confirmed the missiles would be removed from Cuba if the United States promised not to invade the island. The offer was accepted and nuclear war was averted.

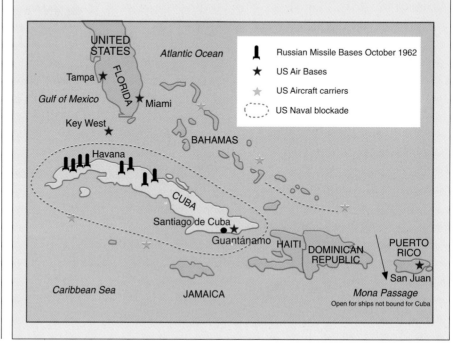

28

The Soviet Embassy building is prominent in Havana, but the alliance between Cuba and Russia has weakened considerably since the end of the Cold War.

RECENT HISTORY

Cuba's recent history continues to be dominated by the hostility of the United States. Cuba's willingness to actively support socialist and Communist movements in Central and South America and Africa, has been seen as a threat to American interests. In the 1970s the Sandinista National Liberation Front, a guerrilla movement in Nicaragua, received weapons and military training from Cuba. In 1975 and 1976, Cuban troops took part in a civil war in Angola in Africa, supporting the pro-Communist side, and towards the end of that decade Cubans also fought in support of Ethiopia's socialist government.

In 1980, Castro announced that those Cubans who wanted to leave for the United States were free to do so. A private armada of small boats and ships ferried thousands of disaffected Cubans to Florida. But the Cuban government also took the opportunity to ship off a fair percentage of its own prison population. In 1987, an agreement was reached whereby some of the more undesirable immigrants were returned to Cuba.

After the breakup of the Soviet Union in the 1990s it can be argued that Cuba no longer represents a threat to the United States. However, the United States' ban on trade with Cuba remains, and the loss of Russian aid, estimated at $3 million a day, has caused the Cuban economy to nosedive.

GOVERNMENT

CUBA'S SYSTEM OF GOVERNMENT is defined in its constitution as "a socialist state of workers and peasants, and all other manual and intellectual workers." Political power is exercised through the Cuban Communist Party, and Cuba is one of the few countries in the world still committed to the revolutionary ideologies of Marx and Lenin. The average Cuban pays little attention to the ideas of these long dead political thinkers, but Castro's influence remains paramount and the loyalty he inspires is extraordinary.

CONSTITUTION

Cuba's 1976 constitution replaced the Fundamental Law of the Republic instituted in 1959. Under the 1976 constitution Cuba is described as a socialist republic in which all power belongs to workers. The state guarantees work, education, medical care, food, clothing, and housing.

The president is the head of state and the government and commander of the armed forces. The Council of State is made up of the president, five vice presidents, a secretary, and 23 other members. The Council of Ministers—the head of state, vice presidents, and ministers—is the chief administrative organ with executive power. It draws up bills, plans developments, and controls national security.

Opposite: **Cubans with their flag.**

Above: **The Capitoleo was planned to resemble the U.S. Congress building in Washington, D.C.**

All Cubans over the age of 16 are entitled to vote.

The Presidential Palace now houses the Museum of the Revolution.

THE NATIONAL ASSEMBLY

The 589-member National Assembly is elected directly by universal suffrage. Candidates are chosen at meetings of a number of work organizations, including the armed forces and student groups. The election for the National Assembly held in 1993 was the first election in which citizens went to the polls and voted in secret.

Eighty percent of the members of the National Assembly are Communist Party members. Since there are no legal opposition parties, there are no opposition candidates. If voters wish to make a protest, their only choice is to spoil their ballot. In the last election, underground dissidents launched "The 'No' Chain" campaign, urging each Cuban to spoil his or her ballot and encourage five friends to do the same. The campaign had no noticeable effect.

The National Assembly holds two sessions a year and also sits for special sessions called by the Council of State. The 31 members of the Council of State, including the president, are elected by the National Assembly.

THE COMMUNIST PARTY

The 1976 constitution guarantees that the Communist Party should remain the only legitimate party in Cuba. As such it is the most important political institution in the country and is described as "the leading force of society and change."

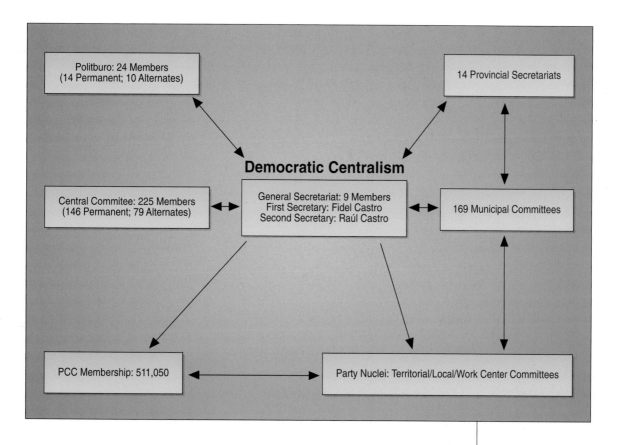

Politburo: 24 Members
(14 Permanent; 10 Alternates)

14 Provincial Secretariats

Democratic Centralism

Central Commitee: 225 Members
(146 Permanent; 79 Alternates)

General Secretariat: 9 Members
First Secretary: Fidel Castro
Second Secretary: Raúl Castro

169 Municipal Committees

PCC Membership: 511,050

Party Nuclei: Territorial/Local/Work Center Committees

The structure of the Party is similar to that of the government. There is a Central Committee of 225 deputies elected at Party congresses. Deputies elect members of the Politburo who form a ruling body. At the top of the pyramidal structure is the Secretariat, and Fidel Castro is First Secretary of the Communist Party.

A Party congress is held every five years. The first was held in 1975. The highlight of such congresses is usually the keynote speech made by Fidel Castro. At the 1986 congress Castro acknowledged mistakes in the over-centralization of power and called for reforms designed to decentralize the political system. At the last congress, held at a time when the Kremlin was ending its one-party rule, Castro again surprised people. This time he railed against the breakup of the Soviet system and insisted that Cuba would not go down the same road.

The Cuban Communist Party structure and membership.

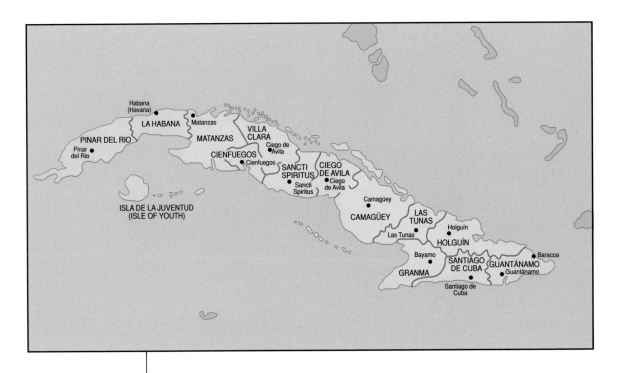

The provinces of Cuba and their capitals.

LOCAL GOVERNMENT

Historically, there were four divisions to the island of Cuba: Oriente in the east, Camagüey, Las Villas, and Occidente. The names are still frequently used, although the country is now officially divided into 14 provinces that form the basis for the administrative and political organs of power. From east to west, they are Guantánamo, Santiago de Cuba, Holguín, Granma, Las Tunas, Camagüey, Ciego de Avila, Sancti Spiritus, Villa Clara, Cienfuegos, Matanzas, the Province of Havana, the City of Havana, and Pinar del Rio. There are 169 municipalities, one of which is a special division, the Isle of Youth.

Local government is based around provincial and municipal assemblies. The more than 10,000 members of municipal assemblies are elected directly, and each municipal assembly is headed by an executive committee. Members of these executive committees form the provincial assemblies. Very few members of the local assemblies serve on a full-time basis. Most members continue with their normal jobs and do not receive any pay for their local government work.

Cuban policemen.

Another important organization of local administration is known as the Committee for the Defense of the Revolution. The neighborhood bodies that form this organization are made up of nearly half the adult population of Cuba and function as the most local form of government. The name of the organization goes back to the early days of the revolution when an invasion from the United States was a very real threat and surveillance groups were established to counter this threat.

FIDEL CASTRO

Fidel Castro making a speech. Castro has been a keen promoter of socialist revolutions in other countries, especially Latin America and Africa, and he has achieved considerable status among Third World nations.

Fidel Castro was born in 1927, the son of an immigrant sugar planter. In 1945, he entered the University of Havana where he received a Ph.D. in law. An exceptional athlete who was considered for professional trials by two American basketball teams, he was also a likely contender to represent Cuba at Olympic-level discus throwing had it not been for his interest in politics.

At the age of 20 he joined the Cuban People's Party. After leading a failed revolution in Santiago in 1953 he was imprisoned and later exiled. In 1956, he landed on the Cuban coast with a small band of followers and conducted a successful guerrilla operation from the Sierra Maestra mountains. After President Batista's fall from power, Castro proclaimed the Cuban Revolution and declared himself prime minister. His popularity increased enormously after the failure of the Bay of Pigs invasion and the numerous assassination attempts on his life.

From many accounts of personal encounters with Fidel Castro, he appears to be a remarkably eloquent and cheerful individual. His ability

INTERVIEWS WITH CASTRO

Since 1959 Castro has given many interviews to newspaper, radio, and television journalists. Recently his views have become particularly interesting because, while many countries have abandoned Communism as an economic and political system, Cuba has steadfastly refused to compromise its basic principles. The following are responses given by Castro since 1991.

On the collapse of the Soviet Union: "All of this points to what a slur it was to say that Cuba was a satellite of the Soviet Union. We have proven that we were not because, although the Soviet Union has disappeared, we have continued to struggle, we continue to pursue our own revolutionary path, we have not become discouraged, we have not surrendered, and we are confronting this harsh test with full confidence in our future."

On the 1993 elections for the National Assembly: "What other country under the siege and blockade that we face, would have the courage to call elections, a free secret ballot where people can vote yes or no, during a period akin to war? Would your country [Britain], with Hitler on the French coast ready to invade, have called such an election?"

On what will happen after the death of Castro: "I don't think that socialism can be identified with me personally: I didn't invent it."

On the United States: "I have never failed to recognize the merits of the American people. One should not forget that the United States was a colony that fought hard for its independence."

On the U.S. Declaration of Independence: "It's really very beautiful. I've always had a great liking and admiration for Abraham Lincoln. The Declaration stated that all men are created free and equal. But at the same time, slavery was maintained for nearly 100 years after that. Which goes to show that the formal statements of principle do not always correspond with the facts."

On the number of assassination attempts made on his life: "If there were an Olympic event in this field, I would certainly have won the gold medal."

On why he wears a guerrilla uniform: "These are my clothes, I've worn them all my life, they are comfortable and simple, they cost little, they never go out of style. But excuse me if I ask you a question: when you interviewed the Pope, did you ask him why he always wears that white outfit?"

Castro's remarkable charisma is evidenced by the number of names he has acquired over the years, including El Comandante ("com-ahn-DAN-te")—the commander, El Caballo ("cab-AHL-lo")—the horse, and El Jefe ("EF-e")—the chief. He is sometimes referred to as just El, and ordinary Cubans call him Fidel even though they may never have spoken to him.

to talk at length is legendary; during the 1960s and 1970s it was common for him to deliver a speech of three or four hours. In 1969, he spoke on television for seven hours non-stop!

Cuba's coat-of-arms, known as the royal palm, is a shield flanked on the left and right by oak and laurel branches. The seascape represents the mouth of the Gulf of Mexico. Hanging between the two headlands is a key, referring to the Spanish description of Cuba as the "key to the Gulf of Mexico." The rest of the shield is divided into two parts. The left half shows white and blue diagonal bars, while the right half displays a royal palm, the national tree, between two conical mountains. The shield is in front of a liberty pole surmounted by a red wool cap, also representing liberty, with a lone white star on its front.

HOW FREE IS CUBA?

On the plus side, the majority of Cubans support a system that, until very recently, provided a standard of living comparing favorably with its neighbors. The government has reduced the gap between the rich and the poor. The present state of deprivation affects all Cubans, regardless of color or class, and despite the harsh times there are no beggars in Cuba.

On the minus side, the Castro government has refused to accept the need for political opposition. Underground groups of dissidents exist and are subject to sudden arrest and imprisonment. The number of political prisoners is not known. Past attempts by the United States to destabilize Cuba gives the government a reason for feeling paranoid and an excuse for harassing those who are committed to peaceful political change.

The Alternative Criterion Group is the collective name for small groups who unofficially function as the main political opposition. Many of its leaders have spent long periods of time in prison.

The present economic crisis tests Cuba's claim to be a democratic, though one-party, state. In 1992, Rapid Action Brigades were formed, largely in response to the growing discontent over shortages of essential items. Demonstrations by citizens were met by force. Young Cubans, who do not remember the pre-Castro dictatorship and poverty, are keen to enjoy the North American lifestyle they see in Hollywood movies.

BACK TO THE FUTURE?

The Cuban American National Foundation, a very effective pressure group of Cuban exiles in Miami, has detailed plans for running a post-Castro government. The Foundation points out that many U.S. corporations are ready to fuel what is seen as an instant $2 billion market. Cuba is regarded as the last undeveloped business market in the Western hemisphere.

McDonald's, the fast-food company, has more than 40 franchise applications on file if and when the Castro government collapses or is replaced.

Those loyal to Castro claim that business interests would return Cuba to a state of economic dependence on the United States. Most Cubans, even those critical of Castro's authoritarian regime, do not wish to see Cuba become a U.S. colony again. Castro loyalists claim that much of Cuba has already been sold to foreign corporations. Stocks and shares dating back to prerevolutionary days are said to be traded and many Cuban exiles are waiting to claim property seized by the Castro government in 1959.

Even if Cuba survives the present economic crisis, there may be a political crisis once Castro is no longer commanding the country. There is no obvious successor and the enormous influence Castro has wielded may well leave a political vacuum when he is no longer the head of state.

The poster exhorts Cubans to be alert. The ability of ordinary Cubans to stoically accept material deprivation has impressed people visiting the island over recent years.

ECONOMY

CUBA HAS SUFFERED ECONOMIC PROBLEMS for many years due to several factors. One is Cuba's dependence on sugar, its chief commodity. Whenever the sugarcane harvest is poor because of unfavorable weather conditions or when the price of sugar drops due to increased sugar production elsewhere, Cuba's export value decreases and this creates shortages in the country.

Another factor is Cuba's loss of Soviet aid since the breakup of the Soviet Union. This includes the loss of the highly subsidized price that the Soviet Union previously paid for Cuban sugar exports. The loss of Cuba's educated elite, who fled Castro's Cuba whenever the opportunity permitted, along with the loss of American investment and knowhow in the early 1960s, hardly helped.

To stabilize the economy, efforts had to be made to diversify it. Yet Cuba has scant financial resources to invest in machinery and factories for new industries. It must also divert some workers from the sugar industry to new industries—a problem in itself, because to pay for the new industries it has to increase sugar production.

To increase its industrial base, the government must court foreign companies to start business ventures in Cuba. It has an uphill task, given its record in expropriating foreign assets.

Opposite: **A Cuban farm worker cuts sugarcane.**

Below: **A resort hotel in Viñales. Tourism in Cuba brings in badly needed foreign currency.**

A worker puts finishing touches on cigars in a cigar factory in the city of Trinidad.

NATURAL RESOURCES

Cuba's economy is primarily agricultural, reflecting the fact that 80% of the total land area is farmland. Although the number of individual farm owners is increasing, most of the farmland—about 70%—is owned by the state. Two Agrarian Reform laws, in 1959 and 1963, set limits on the size of privately owned farms as well as making the government the proprietor of all land in Cuba. The same laws also distributed land to former squatters. Approximately 100,000 farmers, who formerly worked on farms of less than 67 acres, received free title to the land they occupied. All land once owned by non-Cuban individuals and companies was expropriated by the state.

The main crop is sugar. Only Brazil and India, vast countries compared to Cuba, produce more sugar. Coffee is the second largest agricultural export. Tobacco, nearly 85% of which is grown by small farmers, mostly in the northwest of the island, has made Cuba world famous for its cigars, the main form of tobacco exports. Recently, however, the economic

importance of tobacco has declined steadily; now it occupies only about 1% of cultivated land.

Livestock production is also vital to the country's economy and intensive stockraising is practiced on large cattle farms. Other farms are devoted to the production of rice, citrus fruits, bananas, pineapples, potatoes, tomatoes, and sweet potatoes.

An important natural resource progressively developed since 1959 is the fishing industry. Some 50,000 people are employed in the five ocean going fleets that are run as cooperatives. One of the largest fishing ports in the Caribbean has been built in Havana, and a shipbuilding industry has developed there. Other important ports are Cienfuegos and Caibarién.

Cuba is the world's fourth largest producer of nickel, and nickel reserves constituting over 10% of the world's total reserves are found in northeast Cuba. Nickel is now Cuba's largest export after sugar. There are also significant deposits of limestone that form the basis of a small cement-making industry. Other small mining concerns are based around supplies of gold, silver, cobalt, and chromium.

SUGAR IS NOT ALWAYS SWEET

The harvesting of sugar has long functioned as the dynamic of Cuba's economy, and until 1991 the export of sugar to the Soviet Union and Eastern Europe accounted for over 75% of the island's revenue from trade. Cuba's imports were worth $8 billion because of the favorable price the Soviet bloc was prepared to pay. Today, Cuba can only sell its sugar at world market prices and the result is that by 1994 the country's imports amounted to only $1.7 billion.

Since the days of Spanish rule the Cuban economy has been locked into the sugarcane industry. For a long time the industry's high level of profitability was linked to the easy availability of cheap hired labor. After the departure of the Spanish, Cuban farmers became independent owners of sugar farms. Too soon, however, U.S. corporations moved in. When the price of sugar reached an all-time low in the early 1920s large U.S. companies were able to take over near-bankrupt farms, smaller corporations, and sugar mills. By 1930 nearly three-quarters of Cuba's sugar industry was owned by U.S. corporations and the plantation worker found that the European colonial master had been swapped for one nearer home.

Another problem that continues to bedevil the Cuban sugar industry—whether under Spanish, American, or Cuban control—is the unpredictability of drought. A lack of expected rain can seriously damage the value of the eventual sugar harvest.

Opposite: **Sugar mill and refinery about 60 miles outside Havana.**

Below: **An oil rig in Cuba. The country is constantly searching for new energy sources to power its growing industrial base.**

INDUSTRY

In the decade following the 1959 revolution, the entire industrial and manufacturing sector was nationalized. The largest industries are food processing, chemicals, pharmaceuticals, textiles, and clothing. Sugar milling is the chief form of food processing, allowing for the production not only of raw sugar but also by-products like brandy, rum, and molasses.

Even before the collapse of Cuba's main trading partners in Eastern Europe, the government was trying to diversify the country's manufacturing base and reduce its dependence on sugar. Fluctuations in world prices for sugar combined with the adverse effects of a drought led economic planners to actively seek new sources of industrial employment.

At present, over 15% of the labor force is employed in manufacturing and mining. This figure would be a lot higher if Cuba had a larger international market for its exports, as well as the basic energy supplies needed to fuel activities in these sectors.

CUBAN PRODUCTS There is a valuable potential for the production of industrial products, including electric power, paper, footwear, and electronics. Utilizing natural resources, Cuba has grown a base of small businesses producing handicrafts such as dolls made of wood and seeds, wood carvings, jewelry, and leather goods. These find a ready market among tourists.

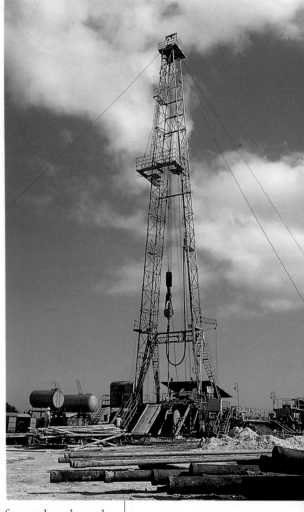

Animal power replaces Soviet-built farm machinery that has fallen into disuse for lack of spare parts.

Cuba's trade with U.S. foreign subsidiaries rose from around $100 million in 1988 to more than $500 million in 1990. The Cuban Democracy Act is designed to cut off this trade.

THE BIG SQUEEZE

The United States imposed the first trade restrictions on Cuba in 1960, a year after Fidel Castro took power; by 1963 these were extended to include a full embargo on trade, the prohibition of all dollar transactions with Cuba, and the freezing of all Cuban assets held in the United States. About 30 years later, new restrictions were proposed. The Cuban Democracy Act of 1992, brought to Congress by Robert Torricelli, Democrat of New Jersey and chairman of the Foreign Affairs Subcommittee on Western Hemisphere Affairs, tightens economic sanctions against Cuba, to weaken Castro and hasten his downfall.

Under the Act it is forbidden for any foreign subsidiary of a U.S. company to trade with Cuba. In addition, any ship that docks in a Cuban port is prohibited from trading in U.S. ports for the following six months. The Act also authorizes the president to "condition U.S. aid and trade relations with other countries that provide assistance to Cuba." This is seen by many as a transparent attempt to intimidate any country that might consider trying to trade with Cuba. The act spells out the conditions necessary to allow normal trade: "When a Cuban government has been elected through free and fair elections under supervision."

The implementation of the Act occasioned international dissent, and Canada and Mexico insisted on their right to trade with Cuba. The parliament of the European Economic Union protested and proposed increased cooperation with Cuba to counter the effects of the Act. The United Nations General Assembly has approved, by an overwhelming majority, Cuba's appeal against the U.S. action.

In January 1989, Cuban workers were busy loading Russian ships in Havana port. With the breakup of the Soviet Union, the situation has changed drastically.

SOCIALISM OR DEATH

Socialismo o Muerte ("soh-see-ial-IS-mo oh moo-AIR-teh")—socialism or death—is the exhortation designed to help Cubans accept the austere demands made upon their national and political loyalty.

When Cuba was able to export the bulk of its sugar harvest to the Soviet Union it could obtain oil, chemicals, machinery, and food at subsidized prices. The loss of these vital imports had a disastrous effect on Cuba's economy and the lives of Cubans. Sugar mills run well below their optimum level because of inadequate supplies of fuel and replacement parts for essential machinery. In the fields sugarcane production is held back by shortages of fertilizers, pesticides, and fuel for harvesters and tractors. Oxen perform the work once done by tractors. Gasoline is restricted for essential purposes. Food, clothing, and electricity are strictly rationed, and meat rarely appears on the average Cuban's dinner table.

Spanish investment in Cuba has risen enormously over recent years. Between 1989 and 1990 it rose from $150,000 to $28 million.

Besides sun-and-sea attractions, Cuba boasts sites such as the El Bar del Medio in Old Havana, one of Hemingway's favorite haunts.

EL TIEMPO ESPECIAL

El tiempo especial ("el tee-EM-po es-spes-EE-ahl")—the special period— is what Cubans call their current period of economic hardship. Faced with an economy close to collapse, the government was forced to introduce radical changes.

In 1993, new legislation allowed private citizens to hold and spend U.S. dollars. This important departure confirms the presence of a dollar black market, supplied mainly by foreign tourists and money sent to relatives by Cubans in the United States. On the black market, the peso trades at around 60 to the dollar; the official exchange rate is one peso to one dollar. Legalizing the use of the dollar is expected to stimulate remittances from abroad, which totalled $300 million in 1992. It will also increase inequalities because, while Cubans continue to be paid in pesos, those able to obtain dollars have access to privileges.

Cuba is also courting foreign investors with a zeal that would have been unthinkable in the past. A host of new joint-venture contracts have been signed, particularly in the tourist industry. The government is studying proposals for a partly foreign-owned bank. It is even considering the possibility of restoring private food markets that would allow Cubans to

TOURISM—AGAIN!

Before 1959, Cuba's second biggest source of revenue was tourism. The island was infamous for its casinos and dubious nightlife and was a convenient vacation spot for wealthy North Americans. After the revolution all tourist hotels and casinos were closed and U.S. citizens were not allowed by their government to visit the island. The tourism industry did not recover until the mid-1970s when Canadians, Latin Americans, and Europeans—especially from Spain—were attracted to the beautiful island that was far less expensive than most of its Caribbean neighbors. Since the late 1980s, increasing the number of visitors has become a national priority. To maximize foreign currency earnings, vacationers are required to use dollars for all their expenses while on the island.

Cuba is being marketed as an ecologically friendly island. It is true that the dire shortage of oil reduces pollution and the reduction in industrial activity makes for cleaner air. At the same time, though, there is little control over the pollution caused by the dumping of by-products from sugarcane processors or the contamination of sea water by Havana Bay's oil refinery and untreated sewage from the capital.

Cuba's main tourist resort area is Varadero, two hours by bus to the east of Havana, mostly financed by a joint venture with a Spanish hotel chain. The government has set a goal of 50,000 hotel rooms by 1995; in 1988 there were less than 8,000. In December 1993, the government allowed gambling on the cruise ship *Santiago de Cuba*, based in Havana, although wagering can only begin beyond the 12-mile limit, in accordance with Cuba's onshore gambling ban.

harvest and sell their own agricultural produce. Such a scheme was in operation once before but was abolished in 1986 when some private peasant farmers and distributors became corrupt and rich at the expense of consumers.

New legislation has also allowed for greater private participation in agriculture and the number of individually-run farms has been increased as a result. During this special period of austerity many thousands of urban workers are being sent to state farms in an effort to make the country self-sufficient in food.

All these changes are designed to strengthen, not dismantle, the framework of a centrally-controlled economy. They also signal a recognition of inadequacies in an economy too dogmatically controlled by the state. If Cuba survives the current economic crisis—more severe a challenge than any faced since 1959—the socialism that emerges may prove stronger and more credible than the one that depended on subsidies from Eastern European countries for its survival.

"Cuba's favorable environmental conditions are a fundamental premise for the development of the tourism industry."

—Fidel Castro, at the Earth Summit (1992) in Rio de Janeiro

CUBANS

CUBANS ARE a mixture of races. Underlying ethnic differences are similarities in temperament that help characterize the Cubans as a nation. They have a reputation for being friendly and sociable. They have a strong sense of national pride and a patriotic belief in the achievements of the last 35 years, but the present economic crisis is severely testing this sense of national solidarity.

ETHNIC MIX

Cubans who are of European, mostly Spanish, descent are classified as Creoles and they make up more than half the population. Cubans of mixed African and European descent are classified as mulattoes. A significant proportion of Cubans are blacks, descended directly from slaves brought from West Africa in the 19th century. Smaller minorities consist of Spanish and Chinese. The Chinese were brought to Cuba in the 19th century when the African slave trade was coming to an end. In the last century it was forbidden for blacks and Chinese to marry, but nowadays all of the different races intermarry. This accounts for the surprising variety in skin tones found among the Cuban people.

Opposite: **A black Cuban family poses for the photographer in the doorway of their home.**

Above: **An easy camaraderie exists among these Cuban children in a playground.**

More recent immigrants to Cuba are political refugees from Latin America. Fidel Castro has always championed socialist revolutions in South America and offered a home to dissidents who have had to flee their own countries. After the overthrow of the left-wing President Allende of Chile in 1973, for example, many Chileans fled to Cuba.

A party of teenagers in Havana.

RACIAL PREJUDICE

An important part of Cuba's identity, as a socialist state, is that everyone has equal rights and opportunities. In most areas of life egalitarian principles are seen to be successfully operating. Very little racism is seen in personal relationships, and in this respect Cuba has made tremendous progress. Racist attitudes do, however, still influence some aspects of Cuban life. And it is a fact that black Cubans are not always treated in the same way as Cubans of European descent.

The higher ranks of many occupations are more likely to be filled by people of European or mixed European descent. This tendency is apparent in the tourist industry where white Cubans are more likely to be employed as receptionists, tour guides, and waiters. Black Cubans are much more likely to be employed as cleaners of hotel rooms or laundry operators. Discrimination also seems to operate in government departments that run the education system and the armed forces.

Young black Cubans are the most disaffected group of citizens. They suffer the same material deprivations as everyone else, but often they claim to be harassed by the authorities because of their color. In a way that is similar to the United States and Britain, the police are accused of being biased when it comes to dealing with young blacks suspected of being involved in criminal activity.

Racist attitudes that do persist in Cuba are a legacy of the past. Before 1959, racism was an accepted fact that pervaded all areas of Cuban life. It was not uncommon for mulatto parents to prevent their children from marrying black people in the hope that this would improve their social and economic opportunities.

Despite Cuba's claim to equality, lighter-skinned Cubans still have the advantage over their darker counterparts in some sectors of the job market.

THE ETHNIC MELTING POT

The proportion of different peoples in Cuba is:

60%	Creoles, of European descent
22%	mulattoes, of mixed African and European descent
12%	blacks, of West African descent
3%	Spanish
1%	Chinese
1%	other minorities

Miami, Florida, has a large population of Cuban expatriates.

CUBANS ABROAD

Before 1959, when grinding poverty was a way of life for many Cubans, the United States beckoned as a paradise. Most Cubans who could afford the expense and secure entry left for Miami. When the Batista dictatorship collapsed in 1959 the people who fled the island were affluent Cubans who realized their privileged lifestyle would not be tolerated by the new socialist regime. The majority of this exodus of about 200,000 people went to the United States. Florida was the most popular destination, and here they formed the basis for a community of Cuban exiles. Other Cubans settled in Mexico and various South American countries.

In 1965, Castro allowed disenchanted Cubans not of military age to leave; over the next eight years another 300,000 Cubans left for the United States. After this, until 1980, very few Cubans left their country. It is only in the last few years that the right to foreign travel has been available to Cuban women below the age of 60 and men below 65. More recently, the permitted ages were 30 and 35 respectively for women and men.

THE FLORIDA CONNECTION

There are more Cubans in Florida than any other U.S. state, more indeed than in any other country in the world. Although there are Cuban communities in New York , Chicago, and Los Angeles, over 60% live in south Florida. Their numbers are increasing as more refugees make the 90-mile journey from Cuba. Sometimes they arrive more dramatically than in small boats and rafts. In 1992, a Cuban plane was "hijacked" by its own pilot, with some support from the passengers, and landed in Miami.

Some Cuban refugees, especially those from the post-revolution exodus after 1959, have settled down as permanent Cuban Americans. Many of them were professionals in Cuba, doctors for instance, and found it relatively easy to establish a new life in the United States. Their children have never been to Cuba. Many of the one million Cubans who have settled in the United States since 1960 are sometimes viewed as reluctant immigrants. A poll of immigrant groups conducted in 1991 asked whether they felt "the old country was better." Cubans were virtually the only group who gave an affirmative answer. Polls of Cuban Americans asked whether they wished to return permanently to Cuba give conflicting conclusions. One poll by Florida International University found that over 70% said they would not return.

Most Cuban Americans who are politically active campaign for the overthrow of the Castro regime. Many believe the United States should help finance an invasion force to topple the Castro government. Many of the Cuban Americans who feel this way have substantial claims on Cuban property and seek to reestablish these claims.

In 1980, in a dramatic exodus of Cubans to the United States, some 125,000 Cubans were ferried from Mariel in Pinar del Rio to Miami. President Carter welcomed them as political refugees. Some of these refugees later returned to Cuba.

Since the early 1990s the number of those escaping from Cuba in small boats and rafts across the Florida straits has increased steadily. "Brothers to the Rescue" are volunteer pilots, mostly Cuban Americans, who fly three times weekly over the Florida straits in search of refugees, which gives an indication of the regular flow of people fleeing the island in small boats. The U.S. Coast Guard says Cuban refugees entering the United States by sea totaled 467 in 1990, over 2,000 in 1992, and almost double that in 1993.

The refugees are accepted as individuals seeking political asylum and put in touch with friends or relatives in the United States. Such freedom is unlikely to continue if the numbers keep increasing. If the Castro regime were to collapse, it is estimated that as many 80,000 Cubans would flee to the United States.

DEMOGRAPHY

Demographic trends reflect the changing economic and social conditions of Cubans. In the years immediately after 1959, the birth rate rose steadily in response to improvements in the standard of living. This was especially the case among low income groups. However, the death rate also increased because a large proportion of doctors left the country. The U.S. trade embargo also resulted in a serious shortage of medicines.

The mortality rate gradually dropped as standards of health improved and new doctors were trained. It is only in the last couple of years that a serious shortage of medicines has again occurred, a result of the economic crisis afflicting the country.

The hard times are also affecting the birth rate, which is also beginning to slow down. This is offset to a degree by the fact that 60% of the island's population were born since 1959, and a high proportion of these people are now of childbearing age.

NATURAL FLAIR

Cuban people are naturally flamboyant and this is seen in the way they dress. There is no national costume, but whenever Cubans dress up they do so with an innate sense of style and exuberance. It may also be a reflection of their sense of pride. The subtropical climate encourages the wearing of light cotton clothes. An open-necked shirt, often worn over cotton slacks, is the typical male dress. Women tend to wear the loose, colorful clothing, often short-sleeved or sleeveless, appropriate to the climate.

The item of dress that comes closest to being labelled a national costume is the *guayabera* ("kway-a-ber-a"), a cotton top that is a cross between a shirt and a light jacket. It was originally a form of male dress dating back to the 18th century. A Spanish tailor in the village of Yayabo, in Sancti Spiritus province, is said to have first promoted its use. It is claimed that the word Yayabo accounts for the name *guayabera*. True or not, there is a definite Spanish influence in the wearing of the *guayabera*. Women add embroidery, as well as buttons and tucks, and it is now worn by Cubans of both sexes.

Above: **Young Cuban women.**

Opposite: **Children waiting patiently as their mothers chat in a candy store.**

LIFESTYLE

IN SPITE OF the current austerity measures Cubans have a lively and fascinating lifestyle. The role of the state is central to many areas of life, but the value of individuality continually asserts itself. The country's ideology stresses duty and communal effort, but the ordinary Cuban has a healthy disrespect for too much authority. Enjoying oneself is still a national hobby. Lifestyles have had to adapt to harsh economic conditions, but adjustments are often made with imagination, good humor, and a sense of optimism. Older citizens still remember the fact that in the 1950s the Havana city orphanages had a specially adapted chute with flaps over the top, allowing parents to safely deposit babies they could no longer afford to keep.

Opposite: **A Cuban woman pressing the family's clothes.**

Above: **Cubans wait in line at a shop. Cuban shops often do not display a sign advertising the variety of goods or services offered.**

ECONOMIC SYSTEM

Many aspects of life are managed in Cuba in a way that is quite different from the United States and most other countries of the world. Until the early 1990s Cuba shared many similarities with Eastern Europe and the Soviet Union. With the economic changes in Eastern Europe, the predominant role of the state in Cuban life now only has parallels in a few other places, such as China and Vietnam.

The economy is governed by the state and not by private businesses. In a private enterprise system, when demand outstrips supply, prices rise. In Cuba, the current shortages of food and most consumer items means instead a widespread system of rationing. In June 1991, bread was rationed to three ounces per person per day and the ration of eggs was

Living standards have fallen by an estimated 50% over the last two years.

reduced to nine per person every two weeks. The weekly ration of meat is three-quarters of a pound, which costs about 50 cents. On the free market, where most rationed items are available at a higher price, the same amount of meat costs about $1.30. Shoes and clothes must last two years.

Long lines are now a regular feature of the Cuban lifestyle. People wait in line not only for meat and bread, but also for bus and train tickets, ice cream, or a new shipment of television sets. The easygoing nature of Cubans means that most lines develop haphazardly and new arrivals simply ask *L'ultimo?* ("lul-ti-mo")—or *L'ultima?* if addressing a woman—to establish whether they have correctly identified the last person in the line. When the line is for a basic food item in very short supply the needy consumers are more disciplined and regulated. Some people wait a long time to be near the front of a line and then sell their position to someone just arriving. Young unemployed Cubans earn some money by hiring themselves out to wait in a line for those who have money but little patience.

With its line of old American models on the road, this Cuban street looks like a movie production set for a scene from the 1950s.

TRANSPORTATION Lines are just one aspect of the hard times now afflicting the people of Cuba. The absence of oil means that gasoline is a scarce commodity, and grand four-lane highways once busy with traffic are now eerily empty. Ponies and donkeys—normally strictly forbidden on a highway—are beginning to venture onto the main roads.

MICROBRIGADES

Before 1959 poverty and deprivation were widespread in Cuba. One manifestation of this was inadequate housing and overcrowding, especially in cities. In the post-revolution years the increased birth rate focused attention on the need for drastic improvements in the provision of housing. One Cuban response was the formation of microbrigades.

Microbrigades are small groups of workers who take time off from their usual occupations to assist with building programs. The workers are a mixture of professional and manual workers of both sexes. The general plan is that 33% of the workforce from a factory or government department is mobilized to construct five-story blocks of apartments, under the supervision of building professionals, while the remaining workforce maintains production levels at 100%.

In urban areas, microbrigades are most likely to be engaged in public housing programs. In the countryside, where living accommodation is not a basic problem, the building brigades are involved in building new schools or homes for the elderly.

The use of these building brigades serves a political as well as a practical purpose. Cuba is intent on constructing the kind of society where all the citizens see it as their duty to contribute to the public good. The present economic crisis has halted all new building programs because of a shortage of raw materials.

CUBAN HOMES

One positive side to Cuba's central planning is that there are no homeless people in the country. Rent is, on average, only about 10% of a person's salary. All housing projects are initiated by the state, but tenants are now able to purchase their homes through installment payments. Owners of larger houses are allowed to rent out sections as apartments. Hardly anyone lives alone in Cuba, so houses and apartments are nearly always built as family homes.

The Spanish style is clearly visible in cities like Havana and Trinidad, where many 19th century buildings are still standing. Residents in some of the older Spanish buildings in Trinidad are forbidden to install indoor bathrooms because of the changes that would have to be made to the original structures. Preserving a building's architectural integrity is not, however, the main reason for with-holding improvements. Many older houses in the cities are crumbling and suffering from a lack of amenities because there is not enough money to finance the repairs.

The style of old colonial buildings finds an echo in the traditional style of many rural homes. Balconies and patios are a common feature of houses in both Spain and the Caribbean generally. The architecture is a natural response to a hospitable climate that encourages people to think of their home as extending beyond the four walls of the house itself. People like to relax at home; sitting on a patio with friends or neighbors comes naturally to Cubans.

Retired people often share their homes with their children, especially if the children are unmarried. The state security system offers workers the comfort of retiring with pension payments of 68% of their salary for the rest of their days. The average working salary is around $150 a month and a university professor would receive about $500, the absolute maximum. Men retire at 60 and women at 55.

Opposite: **Ornately styled colonial buildings in Old Havana.**

Below: **Spacious buildings with well-kept surroundings at the waterfront in Cienfuegos Bay, southern Cuba.**

A WOMAN'S LIFE

Discrimination against women has been earnestly tackled by the Cuban government. It is illegal to discriminate against women in any field of employment, including the armed forces, and husbands are legally bound to do half the housework. Rape is not a common crime in the country; the mandatory penalty for anyone found guilty of the offense is death. The legislation designed to achieve equality for women is enshrined in the Family Code of 1975. This also includes laws for pregnant women, such as extra rations if they work, and 14 weeks maternity leave.

In some industries, such as this clothing factory, women still represent the majority of workers.

EQUALITY ON THE BATTLEFIELD

Castro has often acknowledged that without the help of women in building and maintaining the underground organization supporting the guerrillas in the 1950s, the revolution would never have succeeded. Celia Sanchez, who became his aide in the closing years of the war, was waiting on the beach in 1956 with transport and supplies of gasoline when Castro and his followers landed from the yacht *Granma* ("GRAN-MAH").

Children in school are reminded of the many women who played crucial roles in Cuba's struggles, including Lydia Doce and Clodorinda Acosta Ferrais who were only in their early 20s when they were killed by Batista's police and thrown into the sea. In September 1958, one of the most dangerous battle positions was on the highway between Havana and Santiago de Cuba. The task was handled by the all-woman Platoon Mariana Grajales. Women fought at the Bay of Pigs and some lost their lives there.

Women have a strong presence in the country's workforce, making up 40% of the total. This is possible mainly because the state provides childcare facilities for mothers. Centers of employment always have day nurseries, allowing infants to be looked after during working hours. Especially in the fields of law, academia, and medicine, women have attained the kind of professional success that is more commonly associated with men in most other countries. So strong is their achievement in one area that the government recently had to introduce a quota system to reduce the intake of female medical students from 75% to 55%. This kind of discrimination for men is unheard of in other countries.

Legislative attempts to achieve equality of opportunity for women have however not always borne practical success. The proportion of management positions held by men—over 90%—suggests that women are still disadvantaged when it comes to promotion at work.

Above: **Cuban women continue to serve their country as soldiers. The women in this picture are part of Cuba's military force returning from Angola in January 1989.**

65

MARRIAGE

Older Cubans remember the days when girls of marriageable age only went out when chaperoned by an older brother or relative. Courting began in the local park as girls would walk around in pairs, with arms linked around each other's waists, while boys strolled around some distance away. Courting remained a highly formal affair, subject to parental approval, culminating in a marriage ceremony at the local church.

During the first 10 years after the revolution the number of marriages doubled. The rate of divorce increased eightfold. These dramatic increases reflected the radical changes affecting women and men. Improvements in economic conditions, like the lowering of rents, increased people's purchasing power and encouraged the planning of families. The traditional role of women as homemakers was challenged as more and more women

MACHISMO

While in theory Cuba is committed to sexual equality, there is still a strong macho element in the national culture. In the *machismo* ("mah-KIS-mo") ethic the female role is primarily domestic and submissive to male authority; the male role is to exercise authority and display macho aggression in both private and professional life. In other words, while men are encouraged to exhibit *machismo*, women are expected to conform to opposite values of virtue and demureness.

The present regulation that says it is a man's duty to share household chores is part of a process designed to eliminate *machismo*. Articles 24-8 of the Family Code, entitled "Rights and Duties Between Husband and Wife," are read out by the person officiating at the marriage ceremony. In addition, children are educated in a highly political way that includes an emphasis on sexual equality. Traditional attitudes die hard, however, and many Cuban males would be upset to think that whistling or hissing at a female was anything more than a charming compliment. People joke that adultery is a national sport—for men only.

A complicated aspect of Cuban *machismo*, arising perhaps from its roots in family values, is that it is not something simply imposed by males on females. A joke in a Cuban magazine for girls sums up the paradox. "Your boyfriend is terribly macho," says a girl to her friend. "Yes," replies the other, "aren't I lucky!" Cuban men will readily admit to their cultivation of *machismo*. However, behind the flirting and the showing off, men respect women.

entered the workforce and benefited from the educational opportunities. The role of religion declined, and the government established "Palaces of Marriages" across the country where secular marriage ceremonies were conducted. Public campaigns invited those living out of wedlock to register as married couples. Divorce laws were liberalized, and the process of obtaining a divorce became readily available to all social classes.

Today, the vast majority of marriages are formalized at secular ceremonies. A church wedding is an unusual event. Divorce is easy and continues to be fairly common. This is especially the case when no children have been born to the couple. Birth control is widely practiced and abortions are relatively easy to obtain. Broken marriages involving children are less common, and the one-parent family is very rare.

EDUCATION FOR ALL

Education, from nursery school to university, is free for all Cubans. School transport, textbooks, equipment, and school meals are all provided free by the state. Cuba has the largest per capita teaching staff in the world. There is one teacher for every 39 students; in the United States it is one for every 77 students and in Canada, one per 52. Nearly twice as many Cuban children finish school compared with Latin America as a whole.

Illiteracy has been virtually eliminated; over a million adults were taught to read and write in a literacy campaign that began three years after the revolution. Adult education remains an important part of the national system of education. There are branches of the main universities in all the provinces and more than half the provinces have schools of music, art, and ballet. These facts represent one of the country's greatest achievements, and Cubans feel justly proud of their educational resources.

The most commonly seen school uniform is khaki or blue trousers or skirt, white shirt or blouse, and a red neckerchief. Due to the favorable climate it is not unusual for classes to be conducted out in the open.

Schooling has been adversely affected by the economic crisis. Nearly all the textbooks, while mostly written in Cuba, were printed in the Soviet Union at little cost. The Soviet Union also supplied paper, school equipment, and chemicals for laboratories. These now have to be paid for at full cost, which is another financial burden for the government. Boarding schools for rural students also face shortages in fundamentals like soap and school meals.

Coed schools are the norm in Cuba.

FIRST CLASS EDUCATION IN A THIRD WORLD TOWN

The standard of education available to all Cubans is quite astonishing considering Cuba's third world status. A typical example may be found in the town and district of Baracoa some 700 miles from Havana. It was only in 1963 that the first road to Baracoa town was built. Before 1959 only three primary schools, two of them private, served the whole area. Now there are 132 primary schools serving Baracoa district.

Out of the 82,000 people living in Baracoa town almost 2,000 are teachers, a third of them holding university degrees. One of the four special schools has a student population of 25, divided between deaf students and slow learners who eventually return to the main school system. All four teachers are graduates, trained to teach the deaf. The town also has an adult education system where a group of 15 teachers works with over 600 peasants on basic secondary education.

Adjustments have been made in the wake of the current economic crisis, and there are further contingency plans. "We're using lamps, but we've got our students making coconut butter in case the kerosene runs out," says the Baracoa director of education. "It's all right but it does produce a lot of smoke!"

Girls from the Lenin School in Havana in their light and navy blue uniforms.

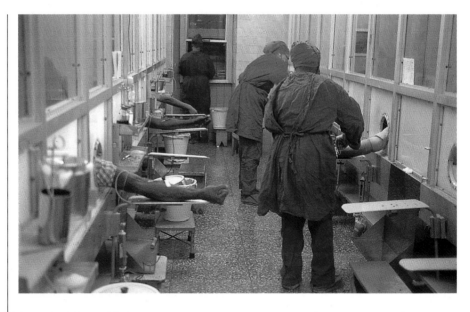

The infant mortality rate in 1959 was 190 per 1,000; it is now 3.2 per thousand, a figure that compares favorably with countries like Sweden and Japan.

Cuban hospital workers take blood samples to test for the AIDS virus. They use their own invention for tests, a small computer blood screener capable of detecting the presence of HIV in blood at an early stage.

HEALTH CARE

Comprehensive medical care, free and available to everyone, is another major achievement of which Cubans are proud. The country has one of the highest standards of medical care in the world. Life expectancy is equal to that prevailing in the United States. With one qualified physician for every 626 inhabitants, Cuba can claim to be in advance of many Central American and Caribbean countries. Neighboring countries make use of Cuba's medical services when their own hospitals lack the expertise and experience to deal with special problems. In El Salvador there is one doctor for every 3,000 inhabitants.

AIDS (known as SIDA in Spanish) is widespread in the Caribbean, although the number of people identified as carriers of AIDS or HIV (Human Immunodeficiency Virus, the AIDS virus) in Cuba is relatively low at around one in 18,000. There are stringent measures in force to prevent the spread of AIDS, including a controversial isolation policy. Sanatoriums are being built in each province for the purpose. Those already in operation started as little more than prisons. Conditions have improved and some AIDS carriers go to work and visit their families. While such a policy would not be acceptable in many countries, the authorities defend it by pointing to the alarming AIDS epidemic in nearby Haiti.

TWO RESULTS OF SHORTAGES

Cubans have long learned to adapt to shortages, with the result that they became environmentally friendly out of sheer necessity. The wheels of old American cars like Chevrolets, for which spare parts are no longer available, are sometimes seen on carts being pulled by a horse or donkey. There are regular cuts in electricity, designed to conserve resources. A typical government building, for instance, will have the supply cut off two afternoons a week and every lunchtime. Working in humid tropical heat without the benefit of air-conditioning or fans is extremely uncomfortable.

Necessity rather than conservation very likely prompted this farmer to use a car tire for his waggon. In Cuba, savings are made by constantly recycling used items.

"AN EPIDEMIC THAT MAY BE TRACED TO POLITICS" This headline is from a story in *The New York Times* in May 1993, reporting on the sudden outbreak of a disease that partially blinded almost 26,000 Cubans. The epidemic began in early 1992, when harsh economic conditions were beginning to take their toll on the traditionally healthy lifestyle of Cubans. As well as gradually losing their vision, the victims suffer from damage to their nervous system, resulting in an imbalance of gait known as ataxia.

The disease has been identified as Strachan syndrome, caused by a serious deficiency of vitamin B1. Tests have shown a deficiency of thiamine, and this vitamin deficiency is linked to the poor economic situation. Only young children are currently provided with an adequate supply of thiamine-rich milk, meat, and eggs. Wheat and rice—the main food items now keeping many Cubans alive—do not contain substantial amounts of vitamin B1.

RELIGION

FORMAL CHURCH RELIGION does not play an important role in the cultural life of Cuba. The Spanish brought Catholicism to the island, but nowadays only about 80,000 Cubans attend Catholic church services on a regular basis. In 1965, Christmas was officially abolished. Far more influential today are religious beliefs that have their origin in West African ancestor worship and animism.

CHURCH AND STATE

Article 8 of the Cuban constitution proclaims that "the State recognizes, respects, and guarantees religious freedom." The Cuban government does not, however, do anything to encourage the influence of the Church in Cuban life. Under the Spanish, the Church was part of the colonial establishment and consequently lost favor with many people. After the Spanish, but long before the revolution, there was growing disenchantment among Cubans about the way the Church failed to champion the needs of the poor who made up the majority of the population. Some priests did, however, speak out against the injustices under the Batista regime. In fact, a Catholic priest served as a chaplain with the revolutionaries in the Sierra Maestra.

After 1959, as the country became more socialist, the Catholic Church became more hostile. In 1960, the rule of Castro was formally denounced in a pastoral letter that was read out at all services. Castro responded by declaring, "Whoever betrays a revolution such as ours betrays Christ and would be capable of crucifying him again." The presence of three priests and a Methodist

Opposite: **The baroque architecture of Havana Cathedral in Old Havana.**

Below: **The Cuban flag is given a prominent place on the altar of a Roman Catholic church.**

clergyman in the abortive Bay of Pigs invasion in 1961 considerably worsened relations between Church and State.

The power of the Church was regulated by the new government. The number of priests was reduced by 80% and church schools were replaced by government ones that excluded any religious education. A visit to the island by the Pope planned for 1991 never took place.

Today, many of the churches do not conduct religious services and function mainly as places of architectural interest. The churches with congregations are usually only open for Sunday services. For a long time it was considered incompatible for a Cuban to hold allegiance to the Church and to the revolutionary State.

RECENT CHANGES

In recent years the government has relaxed its attitude toward the Church, perhaps because the Church has unbent a little from its anti-government position. In the early 1970s another pastoral letter denounced the United States economic blockade of Cuba and communication once more opened between the Church and the State. Practicing Catholics can now become

The peaceful grounds of Cathedral de la Sanctissima in Trinidad. Many churches open their doors for worship only on weekends.

members of the Communist Party. At the end of 1990 it came as a surprise to hear a half-hour church service on State radio, including readings from the scriptures and Christmas carols. Church services are now broadcast on television. Generally, however, the Catholic Church continues to retain a very low profile.

Since 1990, observers have noticed an increased interest in all forms of religion by Cubans that may be related to the increasingly harsh economic climate. The number of baptisms is increasing and more Cubans are beginning to request church burials. An important expression of religious devotion is seen in the pilgrimages to St. Lazarus's sanctuary, just outside Havana. Attendance at Christmas has increased dramatically over the last few years.

A human skull and a bell are part of a voodoo ritual.

AFRO-CUBAN RELIGIONS

The thousands of slaves transported to Cuba by the Spanish brought their religions with them. The Catholic Church was tolerant toward these non-Christian beliefs, partly because the African religions were receptive to some aspects of Catholicism, and a synthesis of sorts took place.

Pedro Augustan Morell de Santa Cruz, a bishop of Cuba between 1755 and 1768, witnessed a rebellion of slaves and saw good reason for tolerating some aspects of African theology. If some tolerance were shown, he thought, there would be less resentment by the slaves and in time their beliefs would wither away. Under Morell, the Christian celebration of Epiphany (January 6) became a festival for slaves where they were allowed to elect symbolic chiefs and perform religious dances.

It is possible that church authorities were misled as to the extent and depth of this synthesis. Catholicism never took deep root among Cubans, while the African religions flourished and spread to non-black Cubans. Today, forms of Afro-Cuban religions are commonly practiced by Cubans of all ethnic origins. Although there are no official figures, it is believed that as many as three-quarters of all Cubans subscribe to Afro-Cuban beliefs. When white Cubans began to attend ceremonies in large numbers there developed a catchphrase to explain their presence: *Yo no creo pero lo repito* ("yo no KRO pero lo rep-IT-o")—I do not believe but I repeat the ritual.

THE VOODOO ELEMENT

Voodoo, the popular religion of neighboring Haiti, also has a presence in Cuba. Its influence can be traced back to the early 19th century when whites fled from a black revolution in Haiti. Many fled as refugees to the eastern Oriente province of Cuba where they settled and continued to practice their belief in voodoo. At the beginning of the 20th century, the sugar industry in Cuba recruited hundreds of thousands of new black workers from Haiti, and voodoo in Cuba was given a fresh impetus.

Voodoo is a blending of Catholicism with traditional West African beliefs and involves the ritual invoking of the voodoo spirit world through magical prayers and rites. Devotees are believed to be capable of being possessed by spirits and sent into a trance. Believers sometimes place voodoo dolls by the side of trees in cemeteries. Their real significance is often disguised by the outward adoption of Christian symbolism, like the sign of the cross, on the dolls.

SOME AFRO-CUBAN RELIGIONS Roman Catholicism is being increasingly challenged by Santería ("san-te-RI-a"), an African religious cult that includes aspects of Catholicism, notably saint worship.

Two other African religions practiced in Cuba are Palo Monte and Abakua. Palo Monte, also known as the Mayombe cult, originates from the Bantu people of what is now Angola. Adherents of this secretive religion are referred to as *paleros* ("pah-LEHR-ohs") or *congos* ("KONG-ohs") and undergo an initiation ceremony. In common with contemporary beliefs of Bantu people in Africa, there is a strong reliance on the power of black magic, and this characterizes many of the rites.

A religion open to males only is Abakua. It originates from Nigeria and Benin in Africa, although nowadays the majority of its adherents in Cuba are white Cubans. Some observers play down the spiritual aspects of the religion, claiming that self-interest rather than theology binds the members together. It has been compared to the Mafia in terms of its influence and methods. An obligatory part of the initiation ceremony once involved the new member killing the first person he met.

There are no established places of worship for these religions, and while they are tolerated by the government, they do not receive any official support. Abakua, especially, is viewed with some suspicion as a potentially subversive group.

In the African Cuban cult of Santería, the Virgin Mary is the *orisha* or saint of the underworld.

SANTERÍA

The literal meaning of Santería is "the cult of the gods" and the religion is traced back to the Yoruban region of Nigeria in West Africa, the original home of the first slaves destined for Cuba. Over the centuries Santería has mixed its Yoruban spirit worship and magic practices with those from other parts of Africa, especially the Cameroons, and Cuba's neighbor Haiti. The most potent mix, however, has been with Spanish Catholicism.

The number of gods and goddesses worshiped stretches into the hundreds, but about a dozen have emerged as more important to contemporary Cubans. The most important ritual associated with Santería is a dance accompanied by drum music. Dance allows the participants to imitate and role-play events from traditional stories about the lives and deeds of the gods. Different types of drums have special qualities, often magical ones, and are associated with certain gods.

The traditional place of worship is the *cabildo* ("ka-BIL-doe"), a cross between a church and a drinking club. While some aspects of Santería's devotional practices are remarkably Christian in character (see box), others are recognizably African. It is not uncommon for mass hysteria to develop at large gatherings, and devotees, convinced of being possessed, may dress in the clothes associated with their god.

ORISHAS

Called *orishas* ("hor-ISH-ahs"), the gods and goddesses are known also as saints. This is a result of the synthesis that occurred when the African beliefs absorbed some aspects of Catholic theology and practice. Christ became Obatalá and the Virgin Mary was associated with Odudua, goddess of the underworld, and acts of homage were made by ritual slaughtering of white chickens. Important deities were closely identified with certain colors. Ochun, or Oshun, was a beautiful goddess whose color was yellow. She was known for her sexual conquests and yet managed to merge with Carida, the Christian patron saint of Cuba renowned for her virginity.

People choose a particular *orisha* to worship and display their allegiance by wearing beads of a special color around the neck or wrist. Like the Christian saints, each *orisha* has its own special date that functions as an anniversary. The anniversary calls for special acts of adoration, and a devout believer keeps a shrine at home and decorates it colorfully on that day. Small symbolic offerings of food are laid at the foot of the shrine, candles are lit, and prayers are said.

Orishas *with specific Christian counterparts include Oya— Saint Teresa, Osain— Saint Joseph, Orula— Saint Francis, Eleggua— Saint Anthony, Ogún— Saint John the Baptist, Shango— Saint Barbara, and Esu—Satan.*

LANGUAGE

THE MOST OBVIOUS LEGACY of Cuba's colonial past is the Spanish language. First came the conquistadores, missionaries, and sailors; then the merchants and farmers. All spoke Spanish and permanently imposed their language on the island. A similar process occurred on other Caribbean islands and in most of Latin America.

Today Spanish is spoken by all Cubans and is also the language of government and commerce. English, Cuba's second language, is taught in all the schools and required for entrance to university.

Until very recently Russian used to be taught in schools, but it was never very popular. Many Cubans learned Russian when they traveled to the Soviet Union to be trained as scientists and engineers.

The growing importance attached to tourism has increased the use and appeal of English. In this sense a cycle has been completed, for before the revolution, English was widely spoken for the same reason. Older Cubans who had been involved in the lucrative U.S. tourist trade are finding that their second language is once more in demand.

Opposite: Political slogans, a powerful propaganda tool, are a common sight in Cuba.

Below: **Cuban boys take the opportunity to earn a little foreign exchange and brush up their language skills at the same time by helping tourists.**

SPANISH PRONUNCIATION

Pronouncing words in Spanish is relatively easy because basically all the letters are pronounced, subject to some clear rules. The letter *h* is never pronounced, so the capital of Cuba is pronounced "av-AN-a." The letter *j* is pronounced as an aspirated (meaning, pronounced breathily) *h,* so the popular male name José is pronounced "ho-SAY."

The same rule applies to the letter *g* when it is followed by an *e* or *i.* For example, the word

gigante (giant) is pronounced "hee-GAN-tay." When speaking Spanish there is very little difference between the letter *v* and the letter *b*, so the word *vino* (wine) is pronounced "BE-no."

CORRECT STRESS Knowing where to place the stress in a word is governed by a systematic rule. Words ending in a vowel or *n* or *s*—the majority of words in Spanish—always receive a stress on the next to last syllable. For instance, the word for president, *presidente*, is pronounced "pres-e-DEN-tay." All words that end in any consonant except *n* or *s* always receive the stress on the last syllable. If a word breaks this rule and is to be stressed on any other syllable, the change is signified by an accent over the vowel to be stressed. Guantánamo, for example, is pronounced "gwan-TAN-ammo," while Guantanamero (a citizen of Guantánamo) is pronounced "gwan-tan-a-MER-o."

One mark above a letter that affects pronunciation is the tilde. This is a small wave above the *n* that appears in words like España (Spain) and *mañana* (tomorrow). It changes the sound of the letter *n* to *ny*, so that the word for tomorrow is pronounced "man-YAN-a."

CUBAN SPANISH

The first Spaniards to settle in Cuba came from the southern part of Spain known as Andalusia. Although centuries have passed since the first Andalusians arrived, their influence on the way Spanish is spoken in Cuba has proved indelible. A chief characteristic of Cuban Spanish is the relaxation of consonants, especially at the end of

words, and the running together of words. While this is a general characteristic of Spanish in Latin America, it is particularly noticeable in Cuba. Visitors who speak European Spanish often find the pronunciation in Cuba more difficult to adjust to than in other Spanish-speaking countries in Latin America and the Caribbean.

In European Spanish the letters *ce, ci,* and *z* have a soft *th* sound. A word like *cerveza*, meaning beer, is pronounced "th-VEH-sah" as if the speaker has a slight lisp. Cubans tend to drop the *th* sound altogether and replace it with an *s* sound, "sir-VEH-sah."

A characteristic of Cuban Spanish is the tendency to drop the pronunciation of the *s* at the end of words. This is becoming increasingly common throughout Latin America. Linguists predict that it is only a matter of time before the final *s* sound is eliminated altogether. It is natural to wonder, then, how the plural is distinguished from the singular. In the case of a word like *la mamá* (mother) it is usually the context that makes it clear whether one mother or a group of mothers (*la mamás*) is being referred to. Both words are pronounced "ma-MA."

CUBAN TALK

English	Cuban Spanish	Pronunciation
Hello	*hola*	"o-la"
Goodbye	*adios*	"ad-e-os," with the final *s* very slightly pronounced
Pleased to meet you	*mucho gusto*	"MOOCH-o GUST-o"
I am hungry	*tengo hambre*	"TENG-go AM-bre"
I don't speak Spanish	*no hablo español*	"no ab-lo es-pan-YOL"
United States	*Estados Unidos*	"es-TAD-os u-NI-dos," with the final *s* of both words very slightly pronounced

"I'm staying!" A street sign to instill patriotism in Cuban citizens.

FORMS OF ADDRESS

In Spain the terms *señor* ("sen-YOR") and *señora* ("sen-YOR-a") are the common forms of address corresponding to Mr. and Mrs. These terms are used in Cuba but are regarded as rather formal; people generally prefer to use the term *compañero* ("com-pan-YER-o") or *compañera* ("com-pan-YER-a").

Cuban surnames consist of two words, but it is only the first surname that is usually used. For example, the name of the country's president is Fidel Castro Ruz, but to Cubans and the rest of the world, he is referred to as just Fidel Castro. The unused part of the surname, Ruz, is his mother's second name.

When women marry, their third name, that is, the second part of their surname, is replaced by *de* followed by the husband's second name. If Miss María Suárez Prieto married Mr. Pedro Raul Maurell, she becomes Señora (Mrs.) María Suárez de Raul. As the third name is reserved for strictly formal occasions, by both men and women, it is usually not obvious from a woman's name whether she is married.

The surname of Señora María Suárez Raul's children would be Raul Suárez.

BODY LANGUAGE

Using body language as a form of expression is an integral part of the Cuban communicative process. It is often used in an almost intuitive manner. For example, when a Cuban wants to refer to Fidel Castro the gesture of rubbing an imaginary beard will sometimes be used instead of his name or title. No ridicule or contempt is implied by such a gesture.

POLITICAL LANGUAGE

Cuba is a highly politicized country, and this is reflected in the use of banners, posters, and slogans to communicate political ideas. Poster art is highly developed in Cuba, usually accompanied by words but equally capable of communicating successfully through visuals alone.

During the 1960s, particularly, the use of posters to communicate with citizens was an aspect of daily life. The images were mounted in special poster stands and periodically changed, in the way that advertising posters are changed in the United States and elsewhere. Posters that were regarded as particularly successful in communicating ideas about political and social issues were reproduced in books and presented on billboards. Giant billboards erected before 1959 to carry advertising campaigns now bear provocative images about international solidarity.

When Cuba faced the threat of imminent invasion by U.S.-backed counter-revolutionaries in the 1960s, the political motto *Patria o Muerte* ("pa-TREE-a oh moo-AIR-teh")—Country or Death—was frequently used to instill a sense of patriotism and solidarity. Nowadays, the threat of invasion has diminished, but the economic crisis has caused the motto to evolve into *Socialismo o Muerte*—Socialism or Death. Only the shortage of electricity prevents the motto from being lit up in neon, in the style of its antecedent.

Street names also bear testimony to political attitudes. In the first year of Castro's rule many changes were made to the names of main streets that dated from the colonial influence of Spain and the United States. This tradition has continued. In 1973, for instance, Avienda Carlos III—named after a Spanish king—became Avienda Salvador Allende to commemorate the socialist president of Chile who was deposed shortly after his election.

In conversation, when a Cuban wants to emphasize a point, the palms of the hand are sometimes smacked together and accompanied by a call of entra ("EN-tra"). It is not an aggressive gesture and is only used in a positive manner. Hissing in order to attract attention is quite conventional and is not an expression of disapproval.

The natural use of body language is also apparent in Cubans' frequent handshaking. In many Western countries the handshake is often a formal gesture of politeness, but Cubans will use it as a measure of their intimacy with the other person. If the relationship is a close one the handshake will often be correspondingly elaborate. Friends of both sexes also greet each other by a kiss on both cheeks.

ARTS

THE RICH AND CREATIVE side of Cuban culture is most apparent in the arts. Cuban music is the most accessible form of art for non-Spanish speakers and together with dance expresses an essential aspect of Cuban art. The visual arts are equally forthright and adventurous.

CUBAN MUSIC

A festive occasion in Cuba not accompanied by music would be unimaginable to Cubans. Listening and dancing to music comes naturally, for Cubans possess a rich musical tradition. Cuban singers and bands have a strong following in Latin America, and many of Cuba's top musicians regularly tour foreign countries. Professional musicians are employed by the State, and highly talented individuals receive the highest salaries.

The unique sound of Cuban music harks back to the music's ethnic origins in the Yoruban and Congolese cultures of West Africa, the original home of the Cuban slaves. It accounts for the distinctive use of percussion instruments and for the strong link between music and dance and the practices and beliefs of Santería.

Cuban bands usually have at least one guitar player, and this points to the other major influence on Cuba's music: the Spanish introduced the guitar and with the instrument came the dramatic, vigorous Spanish flamenco sounds that blend well with African rhythms. Spanish influence also accounts for the tradition of ballad singing.

AFRO-CUBAN MUSIC AND DANCE TERMS

West African influence on music and dance reveals itself in the Cuban music and dance lexicon:

Rumba, Conga, Mambo	Afro-Cuban dance forms.
Guayo	A ribbed wooden instrument played with a short stick. Similar instruments are still used in West Africa.
Bongo drums	African word for the small drums typically found in a Cuban band.
Chequeré	Gourd-like instrument, like the maracas, filled with seeds and shaken rhythmically. It is commonly used in African dances and rituals.
Ekkue	Drum used in African religious ceremonies.
Firma	African religious signs employed in musical performances.

"You have to have a good voice of course, a voice with 'angel,' and you have to have inspiration."

—*Carlos Embale, explaining what makes a good* son *singer*

THE MUSIC OF SON *Son* ("son"), the indigenous dance music of Cuba, goes back at least two centuries to its home in eastern Cuba. The soul of *son* music is African, but the Hispanic musical tradition has contributed to its evolution. The three distinguishing characteristics of *son* music are the rhythm tapped out on two heavy wooden sticks called claves, the solo vocal element requiring improvisation by the singer, and a repeated chorus toward the middle or end of the musical piece.

The wide range of musical instruments accommodated within *son* include the organ, accordion, flute, violin, trombone, and even the synthesizer. One of the lesser known instruments used is the *tres* ("trehs"), a small three-cord guitar. The *tres* produces a delicate, metallic timbre, one of the most recognizable sounds of *son*.

A renowned *son* band is the Septeto Nacional, founded in 1927 by the famous Ignacio Piñeiro, whose lead singer in 1994 is Carlos Embale. The band has a very strong following throughout Latin America and parts of Africa like Zaire.

Son-charanga ("son-car-ANG-a"), the most popular form of Afro-Cuban music, and *son-changui* ("son-can-GWEE") are varieties of *son* linked by the powerful presence of Elio Reve, the founder of the musical ensemble Los Van Van, the leading chart-toppers in Cuba for more than 10 years. Their highly individual combination of trombones and violins, infused with jazz harmonies, has created a new sound that has been christened *songo* ("SON-GO"). Elio Reve is also the most important proponent of *son-changui*. The music is recognizably *son*, but uses a particular drum called *bata* ("BAH-TAH"), more commonly associated with Santería rites. The percussion sound is provided by the usual Cuban array of bongos, claves, and maracas, but the overall sound is far less jazzy than *son-charanga*.

ALL THAT CUBAN JAZZ Cuban rhythms have influenced jazz since its birth, and from the 1930s the effect was especially decisive. The Dizzy Gillespie orchestra's popularity was enhanced by the incorporation of Cuban sounds in 1946. Two years later Stan Kenton, a prominent jazz musician, hired drummers from an Afro-Cuban band to make a hit record, *The Peanut Vendor*. After World War II, New York and Cuban jazz deeply influenced each other. Today, Cuban jazz takes many forms that depend on the major rhythm adopted. Famous names include Chucho Valdés, his group Irakere, and the acclaimed pianist Gonzalo Rubalcava.

Los Van Van, a popular band in Cuba.

SALSA

Salsa ("SAHL-sa") music is derived from *son* and was brought by self-exiled Cubans to the United States, where it is currently enjoying a revival. It is far less pure than *son*, having absorbed extraneous rhythms such as soul and rock, and *salsa* fans are not conscious of its Cuban origin. Cubans discuss music in terms of how *sabroso* ("sa-BROS-o"), or tasty, it is. This may explain the word *salsa* (sauce). The characteristic sound is a combination of fast piano pieces and multiple percussion instruments. If the band is a big one, guitars, horn, and double bass are added. The result is a small orchestra resembling the big bands that dominated the 1950s cabaret scene in Havana. Those who first exported *salsa* include members of such orchestras.

The Tropicana nightclub in Havana is the biggest and most famous in Cuba, with flashy shows reminiscent of the 1950s.

DANCE

Dance is as integral to Cuban culture as music is, and dancing the night away often literally describes what happens when Cubans are out to enjoy themselves. As with music, the origins of Cuban dance are in Africa and partly in Spain. In Catholic-run colonies drum music and dancing by slaves were not regarded as morally unhealthy or politically dangerous as was sometimes true in the Protestant areas of the southern United States. Consequently, the intricate rhythms accompanying religious rituals were better preserved.

The link between music, dance, and religion is especially preserved in rumba, a form of music that originated among the communities of poor blacks in Havana around the turn of the century. It has been called the purest form of African music to have survived in Cuba.

Traditional rumba music takes different forms. The *yambú* ("jam-BU") is a relatively slow dance performed by two dancers. The *columbia* ("kol-um-BE-a") is usually a men's dance and sometimes involves the use of machetes and knifes. It is faster and more exciting than *yambú* and originates from the Matanzas region. The country's most famous rumba group is known as Los Muñequitos de Matanzas.

A tableau from the opera *The Merry Widow*, performed in Havana.

Other forms of dancing popular in Cuba can be traced back to Spain and France. The traditional French country dance known as *contradanza* ("contra-THAN-sa") was introduced from Haiti. A slower Cuban version, equally classical and formal, is called *danzon* ("dan-SON") and is related to the cha-cha-cha. Dance forms like the cha-cha-cha, conga, mambo, and tango are performed with artistic verve in Cuba.

BALLET Ballet is also highly regarded in Cuba. The National Ballet Company ranks as one of the world's most talented dance companies and once had close links with the Bolshoi and Kirov ballet companies of Russia. The most prominent ballet personality in Central America is Alicia Alonso, a Cuban. She studied in Cuba and New York, where she made her professional debut. She was financially unsuccessful in running her own ballet company in Havana in the 1940s and left once again to work in New York. After the 1959 revolution she returned to Cuba and directed the National Ballet Company, which was given government subsidies.

Two other dance companies in Cuba are Camagüey Ballet and Cuban National Dance.

FNL DE VIET NAM DEL SUR
9 AÑOS DE EJEMPLO Y DE VICTORIA
DICIEMBRE 20 1960-1969
Comité Cubano de Solidaridad con Viet Nam del Sur

A Cuban political poster in the graphic revolutionary tradition, this 1960s one supporting the Vietnam revolution.

POSTER ART

The pluralism of Cuban art is best represented in the visual arts. The posters and paintings of native and self-exiled artists demonstrate a unique combination of Afro-American, Indo-American, and Euro-American traditions. During the 1980s there were exciting developments as artists expressed new themes and questioned the centralized state bureaucracy. The contemporary state of austerity in Cuba is not beneficial to such challenging moods.

The period between 1965 and 1975 has been called the golden age of the poster. Artists still express themselves in this medium, as the tradition is an ongoing one, but in the past Cuban posters had a dramatic international impact. This was partly due to the content, which focused on the achievements of the 1959 revolution and stressed national liberation movements around the world. Equally impressive was the embracing of avant-garde traditions like pop art, minimalism, and surrealism. The rigid dogma that was stifling art in the Soviet Union, by imposing simplistic techniques and themes, was publicly rejected in Cuba by Che Guevara, the revolutionary leader from Argentina who worked closely with Fidel Castro. Some of the most celebrated of all Cuban posters are those depicting Guevara.

Surrealism, a European art movement characterized by dream-like images that often appear to explore the unconscious mind, has influenced Cuban painters. A similar kind of movement in literature, known as magic realism, has been very influential among Latin American writers and has also affected the form of art in Cuba. A good example is a poster for a movie, *The Death of a Bureaucrat*, painted by Alfredo Rostgaard. In the picture the bureaucrat's head is replaced by a hand that points up to a gravestone. The poster and the movie satirize bureaucracy and suggest the need for a breakup of centralized power.

PAINTING

One of Cuba's most famous artists is Wifredo Lam, who was part of the post-World War II surrealist movement. One of his works, *La Jungle*, is in the Museum of Modern Art in New York. In paintings, he set out, in his own words, "to paint the drama of my country, but by thoroughly expressing the Negro spirit, the beauty of the plastic art of the blacks." Lam died in 1982, but a contemporary artist, Manuel Mendive, is consciously building on a similar Afro-Cuban aesthetic. His 1982 work, *Untitled*, is an example of his weaving together of African and Cuban themes.

Raúl Martínez is the painter who introduced pop art into Cuba and developed its form. In *The Island*, painted in 1970, he presents a group portrait of anonymous Cuban citizens alongside prominent individuals like Castro, Che Guevara, and the North Vietnamese leader Ho Chi Minh. Its political message is that all Cuban people are equally important, and no one person should have a special heroic status. Martínez also paints posters, and another of his famous works is a call for the end of machismo.

Many Cuban artists work abroad, especially in neighboring countries like Mexico. Most of them are not political exiles and many return regularly to Cuba. An example is José Bedia who explains: "If I am living here during the 'special [austerity] period' I should spend my time looking for food, not paint and canvas."

When modernist art was being denounced by Eastern European and Soviet leaders, Fidel Castro declared, "Our enemies are capitalists and imperialists, not abstract art."

Alejo Carpentier, a widely respected Cuban novelist, was born in 1904 and educated at Havana University.

LITERATURE

Several generations of Cubans grew up learning first European literature and later American literature. Although Cuban literature existed, not many educated Cubans appreciated it.

After 1959, when the revolutionary government took over, Cubans were encouraged to read books with themes of revolution or equality. Students of Cuban literature today are encouraged to read Cirilo Villaverde's *Cecilia Valdés*, a novel about an ill-fated romance between a mulatto woman and a Spanish-Cuban aristocrat.

Contemporary writers, like all other artists in Cuba, work independently but are salaried by the state. The current shortage of paper has severely curtailed publication, but previously a successful novel sold 40,000 to 80,000 copies. This is extraordinarily high for a country with a population the size of New York City.

POETRY

Poetry's wide appeal is shown by the regular publication of poems in newspapers and magazines. The nationalist hero of the 19th century, José Martí, is also a revered poet. Children are first introduced to his romantic lyrics at school, and a respect for poetry is an attractive aspect that most Cubans maintain throughout adult life.

> With the poor of the earth
> I am happy with my lot:
> The mountain stream
> Pleases me more than the sea.
> —José Martí, *The Temple of the Mountain*

Cuba's poet laureate Nicolás Guillén, a mulatto born in 1902, is one of the Caribbean's best known poets. His focus is on social and ethnic justice and his poetry is about ordinary Cubans. A widely read contemporary poet is Nancy Morejín, whose combination of romantic themes and revolutionary commitment echoes the work of José Martí.

A number of literary competitions are held annually, and winning writers are guaranteed the publication of their book. A highly literate population in a remarkably politicized country provides a very sophisticated readership. It also promotes a healthy literary climate that nurtures new writers and sustains established ones.

Important writers include the novelist Alejo Carpentier (1906–1980) and the poet José Lezama Lima (1910–1976). The novels of Carpentier, a former jounalist and diplomat, belong to an era of political ferment and have wide international appeal. They include *Kingdom of the World*, *Explosion in a Cathedral*, and *Reasons of State*. Lima's poetry is more concerned with a search for the roots of Cuban identity. His most important work, *Paradiso*, has been translated into English.

Political thrillers are very popular with Cubans. In 1974, when two writers wrote a mystery thriller *The Fourth Circle*, the first print-run of 80,000 copies sold out within one month. One of the writers, Luis Rogelio Nogueras, later wrote a novel, *If I Die Tomorrow*, that had a plot involving a Cuban secret service agent infiltrating a group of anti-Castro terrorists.

"Unfortunately, reading is becoming an increasing luxury for the Cuban people themselves. ... the country's lack of hard currency made it very difficult to purchase books from other countries. ... Cuban bookshops are closing, converting to other uses or putting up the prices of their dwindling stocks. ..."

—John Pateman, in a letter to The Bookseller magazine, describing a "Books for Cuba Fund" launched in the United Kingdom for Cuban readers

FILM CULTURE

One of the major artistic developments since 1959 has been the successful creation of a thriving film culture. The Cuban Film Institute, with a staff of over 1,000, directs the making of about six films, 10 cartoons, and about 40 documentaries every year. In addition, a weekly newsreel is seen by millions of Cubans.

Full-length movies often have considerable artistic merit, as well as being free of simplistic ideological control. Movies that have been enthusiastically received at international festivals include *Memories of Underdevelopment* by Tomás Gutiérez Alea, *Lucia* by Humberto Solás, and *For the First Time* by José Massip.

ART FESTIVALS

Every February, Havana dances to the sound of the Jazz Festival. Aficionados of jazz from all over the world descend on the city and join over a thousand Cuban fans for a festival of listening, dancing, and drinking rum. Jazz festivals are held all over the world, but the annual event in Havana inspires particular respect among devotees of this type of music. Over the last couple of years, when the festival was in danger of not taking place because of inadequate funds, financial help from abroad has saved the day. In 1992, the famous Ronnie Scott Jazz Club in London gave a helping hand. A non-jazz festival of music is held annually in November at the tourist resort town of Varadero on the north coast. The Varadero International Music Festival is named after the town.

An important art festival, the Habana Bienal (Havana Biennial) takes place in Cuba every two years. It is an international arts festival featuring exhibitions of paintings, other art forms, and conferences, and is an expression of Cuba's commitment and support to Third World cultural development. Latin American artists provide two-thirds of the total work shown.

Cuba also sponsors the annual International Festival of the New Latin American Cinema. It is a prestigious event that brings together filmmakers and critics from all over the world. People come not only to view new films but also to attend conferences and critical debates on film theory and practice. Hollywood figures occasionally attend, and past guests have included Francis Ford Coppola. The festival usually opens in the old-style Hotel Nacional in Havana with Fidel Castro in attendance.

Equally prestigious, but in the field of ballet, is the annual Havana International Ballet Festival. It attracts major ballet companies from all around the world.

Mural adaptation of Raúl Martínez's *The Island* outside a Havana exhibition center.

LEISURE

LIKE PEOPLE all over the world, Cubans find a variety of ways to enjoy themselves when not at work. Athletic games are popular with all sections of society and the government actively promotes sports at all levels. More relaxing pursuits include dancing and listening to music. At home, Cubans enjoy the company of friends and neighbors, and leisure time is regarded as well spent if animated by good conversation.

BASEBALL

Baseball is Cuba's most popular sport. The game was introduced to the island from the United States in the early 20th century, although evidence suggests that Indian tribes like the Cuban Taínos played a ball game similar to baseball. It has been said that the name of the game comes from the Indian name for ball, *batos.*

Before 1959, the best teams in Cuba were linked to U.S. leagues. Scouts of top U.S. teams regularly searched in Cuba for young players to sign. Many turned out to be highly talented players who later made successful careers with major league teams. A Cuban pitcher for the Cincinnati Reds, Dolf Luque, was with the team for more than a decade. In 1923, he had 27 wins and struck out 127 batters. Other famous Cuban players of the period leading up to the revolution include Minny Minoso of the Chicago White Sox and Camilo Pascual of the Washington Senators.

Despite the severing of relations with the United States there has been no drop in Cuban enthusiasm for baseball. It remains the national sport, and every large town has a stadium that fills up for baseball games. The rules are exactly the same as those in the United States, but there are some surprising differences. No fee is charged for admission to a game and fans are likely to cheer teams with cries of *Socialismo o Muerte*!

"Sports are an antidote to vice."

—*Fidel Castro*

Opposite: **On weekends, Cubans gather for their favorite sport.**

Cuba's national team is always a contender for a medal at the Olympic Games. Players like Luis Giraldo and Victor Mesa are well known outside Cuba, and Tony Oliva of the Minnesota Vikings is a renowned outfielder and slugger. There is always a temptation for individuals to leave Cuba and play as professionals for U.S. teams. José Canesco of the Oaklands A's, for example, was born in Cuba in 1964 but now lives permanently in the United States. The high salaries, especially in austere times, are a great inducement.

Sports are encouraged and basketball courts are among the facilities provided.

In Cuba one can always find youngsters playing baseball on the weekends. Every school competes in inter-school leagues, and local community groups organize their own competitions.

PLAYING THE GAME

Cubans engage in many other games besides baseball in their leisure time. Basketball comes a close second in popularity.

A tradition of playing chess is still upheld in Cuba. A youngster may first learn the game in junior school, and public chess tables in parks are often used for games between senior citizens. During the 1920s one of the few international players who successfully competed with the Russian master players was José Raul Capablanca.

Soccer has not caught the imagination of young Cubans, but is actively encouraged by the government. It is so identified with Latin America that Cuba's relative lack of interest in the game seems an anomaly.

Tennis, squash, wrestling, fencing, swimming, rowing, and volleyball are some other popular sports usually first encountered in school. Wrestling and fencing are particularly popular, and on weekends there is usually a match in a town gymnasium. Even a small town has at least one gymnasium and often a temporary ring is set up in a town square to host a local tournament. Horseracing is also popular, but since gambling was outlawed in 1959 few engage in it.

A three-walled court game enjoyed immensely by players and spectators alike is *jai alai*, which came to Cuba from the Basque region of Spain. It is a very fast game, for two or more players, depending on quick reflexes and speed. Using a 2-foot wicker basket strapped to the hand, players try to hit a small hard ball against the front wall so that their opponents are unable to return it and thus lose a point.

Athletics, along with baseball and boxing, has made Cuba internationally famous. National teams regularly take first place in the Central American and Caribbean Games, and are often the favorites to win events at the Pan American Games. The highlight of Cuba's international presence in sports came in 1991 when it hosted the Pan American Games. National teams from North and South America, including the United States, participated. Cuba can also be guaranteed to return from the Olympics with a cluster of gold, silver, and bronze medals. Past Olympic stars include Luis Mariano Delis in the discus event, Maria Caridad Colon in the javelin event, and Alberto Juantorena in track races. The current world records for the high jump and the deepest unaided dive are held by Cubans.

During the 30 years of close economic and cultural cooperation with the Soviet Union, chess retained a high status in Cuba.

THE ART OF RELAXING

The art of relaxing is an attractive aspect of Cuban culture that finds expression in a variety of ways. A common sight on the verandah or balcony of a Cuban home is a rocking chair. People like to sit in the comfort of their homes and pass the time of day with like-minded neighbors or family acquaintances. Friendship and friendly conversation are highly regarded.

Even more emblematic of contentment is the picture of a relaxed individual seated in a comfortable rocking chair and smoking a Cuban

BOXING

A pugilistic tradition in Cuba existed before 1959, when it was mainly the sport of middle- and upper-class men. After the revolution, when the sport was nurtured by the state and made available to all classes, its popularity increased. Over the years Cuba has produced some outstanding boxers, including Chocolate Kid, Gavilan Kid, and Benny Parets. The most successful was Teofilo Stevenson, who was three times Olympic heavyweight champion—in 1972, 1976, and 1980.

As in other sports in Cuba, there is no clear-cut distinction between amateur and professional players. There are no professional sports people who work full-time as private individuals and negotiate sports or publicity contracts. However, the government attaches a lot of importance to sports, both as a form of fitness and leisure as well as a source of national pride and achievement, and talented individuals are encouraged to devote themselves full-time to a particular sport. During this time they receive a salary and in many respects function as professionals. After his initial success, this was the case with Stevenson.

Boxing is first introduced to young boys at school. Those who show skill and interest are usually encouraged to train by preparing for a local tournament. The country's major boxing competition is the Giraldo Cordova Cardin Tournament, and leading boxers are expected to prove themselves at this annual event.

cigar. The enjoyment of a fine cigar is regarded by tobacco addicts as deeply satisfying, and Cubans are blessed—as well as cursed, in terms of the damage to their health—by ready access to the best cigars in the world. Fidel Castro was a dedicated smoker for many years; he was invariably featured holding a huge cigar in his hand or mouth. In his own words, "after a truly heroic struggle," he managed to quit the habit, but for many Cubans leisure time without a cigar is unthinkable.

The most popular type of cigar is known as a torpedo—about half an inch thick, four inches long, and closed at both ends—and is very inexpensive. Cigars are smoked mainly by men and can last for an hour or more. Cuban cigars, especially the better quality ones that sell for $20 each, used to be very popular in the United States but can no longer be sold there.

Cubans pass the time of day sitting in the doorway, observing passers-by, and simply chatting.

CUBAN CIGARS

The Taino Indians smoked tobacco and passed the habit on to the Spanish settlers, who in turn introduced the idea to Europe. As smoking became increasingly popular and fashionable, the foundations for Cuba's cigar industry were laid. The reputation for excellence associated with Cuban cigars is unrivaled anywhere in the world. Famous personalities like the American writer Ernest Hemingway, who lived for years in Cuba, extolled their virtues. Other famous Cuban cigar addicts include the American comedian Groucho Marx and the British war leader, Prime Minister Winston Churchill.

Nowadays the majority of cigars are machine-produced, but rolling a cigar by hand is still a highly regarded skill. All cigars bear a colored ring that denotes their quality. Cuban men choose a cigar because of its strength and flavor. The word *oscuro* ("os-KUR-o") means dark, but when applied to cigars it means black and very strong; *maduro* ("mad-UR-o") means ripe, and this describes a brown-black cigar with full-bodied flavor; *colorado* ("kolo-RAD-o") means red, and is a reddish-brown, aromatic cigar; *claro* ("KLAR-o") means clear, and denotes a mild-flavored cigar.

Cigar aficionados also claim that the size and shape of a Cuban cigar affect its flavor. Apart from the very popular torpedo, named after its shape, there is the corona cigar with straight sides and one end closed. The perfecto is cylindrical and tapered, with a half-pointed head.

Cigar factories have a tradition of entertaining and educating cigar makers as they work by having readers recite passages from books. Another tradition is that employees smoke freely as they work and take home a couple of cigars each day. The average life expectancy in Cuba is 74, but it is a lot shorter for cigar makers.

A NIGHT OUT

A *Casa de la Trova* ("KAS-a de la TRO-ba") is a cross between a bar, a dance hall, and a small concert hall. They are open from around 9 p.m. to midnight and are very popular on weekends when they also are open during lunchtime. Most large towns and cities have a *Casa de la Trova*.

A *trova* is a classical ballad. In times gone by, troubadours traveled from town to town to recite their ballads to the accompaniment of music. Traditional troubadours are still to be found—Pablito Alminan is a famous name that guarantees a packed house—but nowadays the range of songs and music is far wider. The *nueva trova* ("new-ABE-a TRO-ba") has introduced post-revolution themes into the songs, and there is a blues version of the *trova* known as *filin* ("FIL-in").

A lot of entertainment available to Cubans in their leisure time is free of charge. There is no admission fee to attend a sports event or enter a *Casa de la Trova*. Places that do charge admission, such as the cinema and theater, are not run as profit-making businesses. The cost of a ticket to see a film or a play is a far smaller proportion of a person's income than it is in the United States or Europe. As a consequence, cultural establishments like theaters are patronized by a wide cross-section of the population.

Perhaps for this reason, the distinction between highbrow and popular culture does not apply in Cuba. Places of entertainment that are often associated with particular income levels in other countries are frequented by Cubans of all classes.

Young Cubans get into the swing of things at a dance.

FESTIVALS

FEW ASPECTS OF LIFE remained the same after the flight of Batista on January 1, 1959. The government headed by Fidel Castro abolished many of the public holidays and replaced them with new ones that commemorated important events in the country's history.

The most dramatic consequence of these changes was the demise of religious festivals that had once played an important role in the social life of Cubans. Christmas Day, for instance, is no longer a public holiday and Christmas celebrations are discouraged since it often coincides with the sugarcane harvest time.

The Cuban desire to celebrate was not quashed by the changes. Quite the opposite, for the new holidays and festivals celebrated achievements important to all Cubans. Although the present climate of austerity has made it impossible for people to spend as much money on celebrations as they did previously, the spirit of enjoyment remains undiminished.

REMEMBERING THE NATIONAL REVOLUTION

Havana and Santiago de Cuba mount the most colorful celebrations for Cuba's major annual festival on July 26. Cubans pour into these cities from the countryside to join in the festivities. For weeks before, people are busy preparing fantastic costumes and making the floats that form the highlight of the parades. Across the island, groups of people based around a place of work, an organization, or a residential district strive to produce the most flamboyant and eye-catching displays. A sense of pride accompanies these efforts and tremendous enthusiasm is generated.

Opposite: **A veteran shoulders a flag during the first of May Labor Day march. Everyone participates, including women and children.**

Above: **Children at an art competition. Such events are held on anniversary holidays so that participation is at many levels.**

Dances form an essential part of the celebrations. While some dance troupes are professional, the majority are formed by local groups that practice and rehearse with musicians. Dancing and music are integral parts of Cuban culture enjoyed by young and old. Even when economic conditions are bad, Cubans come out on July 26 to sing and dance and enjoy themselves. Traditionally, an excess of food accompanied the street parties, but sadly this is no longer possible. If the Cuban economy does not recover, the street stalls busy dispensing barbecued pork and goat, selling whistles and firecrackers to children, and maintaining a plentiful supply of rum and beer will soon be only a fond memory.

CARNIVAL

The July 26 Remembrance of the National Rebellion holiday coincides with a traditional carnival that goes back a long way in Cuban history, as far back as 1493, when Christopher Columbus visited Cuba a second time, bringing sugarcane from the Canary Islands.

Before the advent of machinery, all the sugarcane had to be cut by hand using wide-bladed machetes; it was a back-breaking and exhausting occupation. Once the cane was cut, the workers could enjoy a period of rest, and because this was the time they received their wages, it was natural to celebrate.

The workers on the sugar plantations were originally all slaves from Africa, and the dances and music of carnival time can be traced back to traditional tribal festivities from West Africa. Havana and Santiago de Cuba are the most important places where these traditional celebrations are actively preserved. In Santiago de Cuba there is even a museum devoted to preserving memories and artifacts connected to the songs and dances of the July carnival.

Sadly, there has been no major carnival festival since 1990. There is simply not enough money to justify what is, by definition, a period of license and excess. A carnival for the benefit of tourists takes place in the capital over the weekends of December and January, but bears little resemblance to the festival it imitates.

Cubans—some in Castro beards, and at least one wearing the M.26.7 armband—salute their leader at an anniversary march.

Obviously enjoying their break from the school routine, these young Cubans are organized into flag-waving contingents for the celebration of political anniversaries.

PUBLIC HOLIDAYS

July 25–27 is by no means the only occasion when Cubans let their hair down. There are nine other national holidays (see the box below), all of which have a political significance. These days are marked by a mixture of public speeches and partying. Political leaders like Fidel Castro and his brother Raúl deliver keynote speeches to vast crowds of supporters. Such speeches are usually held in large open spaces, like the Plaza de la Revolucion in Santiago de Cuba. The atmosphere at these gatherings

CALENDAR OF HOLIDAYS

January 1	Anniversary of the Victory of the Revolution/New Year
January 28	Birthday of José Martí
February 24	Beginning of the 1895 Revolution
March 13	Anniversary of attack on Presidential Palace
April 19	Bay of Pigs Victory
May 1	International Labor Day
July 25-27	Remembrance of the National Rebellion
October 8	Anniversary of the death of Che Guevara
October 10	Anniversary of the start of the 1868 War of Independence
December 2	Anniversary of the landing of the *Granma*

COMPARSA

A *comparsa* ("kom-PAR-sa") is a theatrical term that covers the dance and music, as well as the performers, associated with a carnival. Traditionally, members of a community got together and organized a *comparsa* as their contribution to the local carnival. After weeks of rehearsal, the *comparsa* was ready for the public and took its part in the grand parade that wove its way through the town center.

While large-scale carnivals are no longer a regular feature of Cuban life, *comparsas* still contribute to special events on public holidays. The tradition of careful rehearsals to ensure perfect timing on the day of performance is still adhered to. A sense of pride and a competitive spirit accompany a *comparsa*. This goes back to the days when every big carnival included a competition for the best *comparsa*, judged by a local committee. The winning *comparsa* was the one displaying the most imaginative combination of costumes and dance.

is genuinely festive. Both before and after the speeches the crowds are entertained with song, dance, and music. In the evening, parties are organized both outside and in people's homes. Until recently there was always plenty of food and drink to contribute to the party atmosphere.

Public holidays are also occasions for families to come together. January 1 is the most important day of the year in this respect. The first day of the year happens to coincide with the date of Batista's departure from Cuba and so it functions as an anniversary of the birth of the new regime. Notwithstanding its political significance, New Year's Day has always been a special day in Cuba. The last day of the year, December 31, is not an official holiday, but it tends to function as one because so many people take the day off work to prepare for parties that night.

Fidel Castro's speech is an essential part of the Anniversary of the Revolution celebrations.

"For our country we will rise!" declares this sign commemorating the February 24 uprising of 1895.

FEBRUARY 24

Every February, Cubans are reminded of an important anniversary through large posters commemorating the anniversary of the Second War for Independence, which began on February 24, 1895.

Plans for the February 24 rebellion were laid as early as January 5, 1892, when José Martí established the Cuban Revolutionary Party in New York, where he lived in exile. He and other exiled rebel leaders held several meetings in Jamaica and Costa Rica, and completed their plans on Christmas Day, 1894. On the appointed day, February 24, uprisings began all over Cuba. The war lasted a few years. It cost the lives of Cuba's most colorful revolutionaries, but ended in the creation of the Republic of Cuba, on May 20, 1902.

Churches are the focus of activity on special festivals like Christmas, when a Christmas tree, artificial snow, and Christmas lights adorn the facade and draw attention to a crèche.

RELIGIOUS DAYS

Traditional religious festivals have either been completely abandoned or absorbed into days of secular celebration. January 6 used to be the celebration of the Feast of Kings, commemorating the day when the Three Kings brought gifts to the baby Jesus. Parents bought small surprise gifts for their children and presented them on the morning of January 6. Although the day now only has special significance for the small minority of Christians in the country, the tradition of exchanging gifts has not completely died out. Nowadays, though, gifts are given and received on July 26.

Before 1959 the most important religious festival was Holy Week, the week before Easter. In 1965, Holy Week was changed to Playa Giron Week and became the focus for periods of mass voluntary labor. Playa Giron is a small village very close to the site of the abortive Bay of Pigs invasion, which took place

over the Easter period in 1961. In 1969, the Easter period became the Playa Giron Month, part of the promotion for a big increase in the country's production of sugar. Then it became the Playa Giron *Quince* ("kin-th"), meaning 15, to signify a two-week period of communal effort.

FOOD

IN COMMON WITH other aspects of the country's culture, the food of Cuba reveals the dual influence of Spain and Africa. From these two very different culinary traditions, combined with locally available ingredients, a distinctive food style has emerged. Unfortunately, the current economic situation has had a dire effect on the supply of essential food items. Rationing is a way of life for all Cuban households and providing basic meals for everyone has become a national priority.

Opposite: **Large bunches of bananas, plentiful in subtropical Cuba, are loaded onto a truck.**

Above: **A sign at the entrance to a crocodile farm illustrates a Cuban folk belief in the aphrodisiacal property of crocodile meat.**

CUBAN TASTES

Cuban tastebuds are not as attuned to hot food as neighboring Latin American countries. There is a partiality for spicy tastes but compared, say, to nearby Mexico the result seems mild. Notwithstanding, a pork chop, for instance, would never be prepared without a mixture of different spices being fried at the same time. Beans of various sorts are a regular favorite; *congri* ("KONG-gree") is made from kidney beans, but black and white beans are also used.

Before the current shortages made any sort of meat expensive, a favorite meat was chicken. Crocodile meat is sometimes eaten and the taste, somewhere between that of chicken and pork, is quite unexotic. Turtle meat is used to prepare stews and soups. Pizzas are very popular as a quick lunchtime meal.

RICE WITH EVERYTHING

The most basic Cuban food item is rice. It forms the staple of most meals, and is commonly served with beans. *Moros y cristianos* ("MO-ros e kris-te-AN-os")—Spanish for Moors and Christians—is the name given for a very popular dish of white rice and black beans cooked together. The Moors were Muslim Arabs who exerted considerable influence over southern Spain for centuries. Another rice dish that is as popular in modern Spain as it is in Cuba is *arroz con pollo* ("ar-OSS con PO-LIO"), chicken with rice.

Picadillo ("pika-DIL-o"), Spanish for minced meat, uses ground beef mixed with green peppers, onions, tomatoes, and olives. Raisins are often mixed in with the rice and sometimes a fried egg is laid over the rice.

A typical Cuban dinner table usually holds a white mound of rice.

COOK A CUBAN MEAL

Moros y Christianos

This is Cuba's unofficial national dish. There are different versions, depending on the type of beans and spices used. The following recipe is a simple, standard one.

2 tablespoons olive oil	salt
1 chopped onion	pepper
1 clove garlic, minced	8 oz. cooked black beans
1 green pepper, sliced	6 oz. rice
2 tomatoes, chopped	³/₄ pint of cold water

Heat the olive oil in a saucepan and add the onion, garlic, and pepper. Sauté until tender. Mix in the tomatoes and stir until a thick consistency is reached. Season with salt and pepper and stir in the beans. Add rice and water. Cover the saucepan and cook gently until the water has been absorbed. Serve with a fried egg over the rice and/or plantains.

Pollo a la pepitoria

Pollo a la pepitoria ("PO-LIO a la pepi-TOR-ia") is a traditional chicken dish from the Oriente province, served with onions.

salt	2 lb. onions, sliced
pepper	bay leaf
3 tablespoons plain flour	6 tablespoons white wine
4 lb. chicken, cut into small pieces	2 eggs, beaten
4 tablespoons oil	

Add salt and pepper to flour and place in a paper or plastic bag. Shake each piece of chicken in the bag to coat. Add to gently heated oil in a frying pan. Sauté the chicken until golden on both sides and then remove to a saucepan. Add the onions to the frying pan, using fresh oil if necessary, with a touch of salt. Add the bay leaf and wine and cook for a few minutes. Pour over the chicken and simmer for about 45 minutes.

Add some sauce from the saucepan to the beaten eggs, mix well, and cook until thick without boiling. Pour sauce over the chicken pieces and serve with rice.

Rural Cubans are fortunate in having ready access to home-grown fruit to supplement their diet. The enormous variety available includes avocado, banana, coconut, custard apple, guava, mango, papaya, pineapple, plantain, wild fig, and citrus fruits like orange, lime, lemon, and pomelo.

It's hot, waiting in line for a bottle of water.

WAITING FOR FOOD

One of the most distressing sights in contemporary Cuba is the line of people patiently waiting for their rations of food outside a shop. The supply and distribution of food has become increasingly erratic, and whenever a shop receives a fresh delivery, the news circulates in a very short time. A line quickly forms and remains until the last of the food has been sold.

Long lines are also a feature of restaurants and food kiosks. Cubans wait in line for even simple dishes like pizza slices and hamburgers, now a monotonously regular part of the Cuban diet. A pizzeria usually opens for a couple of hours each day, to coincide with meal times, and the only way a person can be sure of a meal is by waiting in line. An average restaurant may require a wait of three hours. Patrons collect a ticket from the door, establish the average waiting period and return later to wait for their number to be called.

The average tourist who visits Cuba rarely sees the reality of the severe food shortages. Because tourism is such an important source of foreign currency, no effort is spared to ensure a plentiful supply of food to the beach resort areas that attract a high proportion of visitors. These well-supplied restaurants are too expensive for Cubans.

Cubans can circumvent the long lines by way of the black market. For a period during the 1980s private markets were allowed to operate, and while the government is considering whether to allow their return, they continue to operate illegally. An increasing number of Cubans find it necessary to buy food on the black market to make up for the deprivations imposed by the rationing system. There are also black-market restaurants where Cubans who can afford the higher prices go to enjoy more fulfilling meals than those available in the state-owned restaurants and cafeterias. The typical black-market restaurant is usually a room in a private house where patrons do not have to join a line and where meat is always served.

A rum bottling factory in Piñar del Rio.

CUBAN DRINKS

The most popular alcoholic drink at social and festive occasions is rum. The drink is distilled on the island and, until very recently, was widely available. Nowadays, the rum and beer produced on the island is mainly for export or tourist consumption.

The lively *cervecerías* ("ser-beseh-RIA-as"), the equivalent of a bar or pub once found in almost every town, are now rarely open, and the production of drinks for domestic consumption has been drastically curtailed. The same is true even of the *guaraperas* ("guar-a-PEAR-as"), bars selling drinks of freshly pressed sugarcane. Ironically, the juice of one crop that Cuba can produce in abundance is no longer available to the Cuban people. There was a time when populous places like train and bus stations attracted mobile stalls dispensing sugarcane juice and a pineapple-based drink known as *piña fria* ("PIN-ya FREE-a").

Coffee is the most popular hot drink. It is drunk from tiny cups and is often sipped with ice water. Unlike regular North American coffee, it is quite thick and syrupy. Every town has its share of kiosks and stalls serving only coffee, and many customers bring their own cups to be filled, often improvised from cut-down beer cans.

The most popular tea in Cuba is the herbal variety. Many towns have shops specializing in the preparation of herbal drinks. The dark, orange pith of the tamarind pod, for instance, produces a popular beverage after it has been soaked in sugary water for three or four days. The pod of the

GOOD AND NOT-SO-GOOD RUM

Rum is derived from sugar and, not surprisingly, has been distilled in Cuba for a long time. During the buccaneering days of the pirates, the galleons that sailed from the Caribbean to Spain were preyed on for their supplies of Cuban rum as well as gold.

The first official distilleries were established in the second half of the 18th century, and Cuban rum soon established itself as superior in quality to many other Caribbean brands. Today, the famous Santa Cruz del Norte distillery near Havana, the oldest in the Americas, produces not only prestigious rums but also a number of other exotic drinks. Liqueurs are produced from guavas, oranges, mangoes, pineapples, plums, papayas, and cocoa.

There are more than half a dozen rum factories in Cuba producing different types of rum. The quality brands are mainly destined for export; the bottles that do stay on the island end up in tourist bars and the shops known as hard currency stores where the only currency accepted is the U.S. dollar. The rum consumed by the average Cuban is known as *aguardiente* ("agwar-th-EN-te").

The younger the rum, the lower the price and the more raw and unpalatable the taste. The least expensive is known as *tres años* ("TRES AN-yos")—Spanish for three years—because this is how long it takes to produce. The next best brand is known as *cinco* ("SINK-ko") *años* because it is five years old. There is also a seven-year-old version.

Key (Cayo) Largo and Havana are two Cuban places that spell nostalgia and romance to foreigners. Both the rum label—Havana Rhum—and the tourist brochure sell this popular image of Cuba.

tropical African baobab tree is also used in a herbal drink.

Herbal drinks can be traced back to Africa where their medicinal properties were the source of their popularity. Nowadays, the scarcity of simple pharmaceuticals like aspirin and cold tablets has prompted a renewal of interest in traditional herbs.

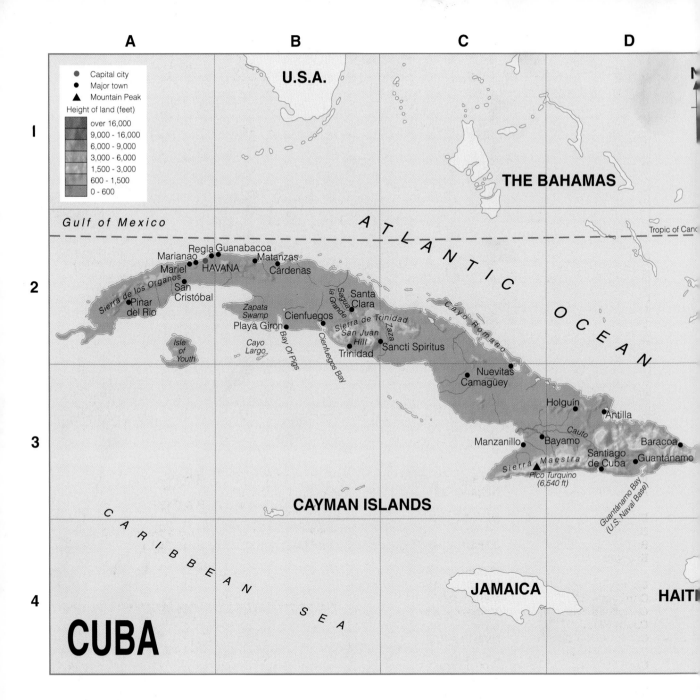

U.S.A.

THE BAHAMAS

I

Gulf of Mexico

A T L A N T I C

Tropic of Canc

2

Marianao Regla Guanabacoa
Mariel   HAVANA Matanzas
San   Cárdenas
Cristóbal
Sierra de los Organos
Pinar
del Rio

Santa
Clara
Sagua la Grande
Zapata Swamp
Cienfuegos
Playà Giron
Cayo Largo
Bay Of Bay Pigs
Cienfuegos Bay
Sierra de Trinidad
San Juan
Hill
Trinidad
Sancti Spiritus
Zaza
Cayo Romano

O C E A N

Isle
of
Youth

3

Nuevitas
Camagüey

Holguín
Antilla

Manzanillo
Cauto
Bayamo
Baracoa
Santiago
de Cuba
Guantánamo
Sierra Maestra
Pico Turquino
(6,540 ft)
*Guantánamo Bay
(U.S. Naval Base)*

CAYMAN ISLANDS

C A R I B B E A N

S E A

4

JAMAICA

HAITI

CUBA

Legend:
- ● Capital city
- ● Major town
- ▲ Mountain Peak

Height of land (feet)
- over 16,000
- 9,000 - 16,000
- 6,000 - 9,000
- 3,000 - 6,000
- 1,500 - 3,000
- 600 - 1,500
- 0 - 600

A   B   C   D

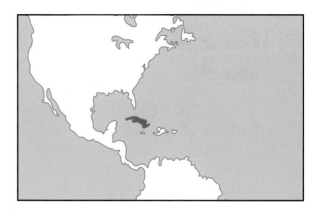

QUICK NOTES

LAND AREA
44,218 square miles.

POPULATION
11 million.

CAPITAL
Havana (La Habana).

MAJOR CITIES
Santiago de Cuba, Camagüey, Holguín, Guantánamo, Santa Clara.

HIGHEST POINT
Pico Turquino (6,540 feet).

MAJOR RIVER
Cauto (150 miles).

FORM OF GOVERNMENT
Socialist Republic.

NATIONAL FLAG
Five equal horizontal stripes, of blue, white, blue, white, and blue, with a red triangle containing a white five-pointed star.

OFFICIAL LANGUAGE
Spanish.

MAIN EXPORTS
Sugar and sugar products, agricultural products, minerals, tobacco products, fish.

MAIN IMPORTS
Mineral fuels and lubricants, machinery and transport equipment, manufactured goods, food and live animals.

CURRENCY
1 Cuban peso = 100 centavos. Official rate of exchange: US$1= 1 peso (unofficial rate US$1 = 40 pesos).

MAIN RELIGION
Roman Catholicism.

IMPORTANT ANNIVERSARIES
January 1, Anniversary of the Victory of the Revolution.
July 25–27, Remembrance of the National Revolution.
December 2, Anniversary of the landing of the *Granma*.

LEADERS IN POLITICS
Fidel Castro Ruz (President since 1959).
Raúl Castro Ruz (Minister of Defense).

LEADERS IN THE ARTS
Alicia Alonso (ballet).
Raúl Martínez (artist).
Wilfredo Lam (artist).
Alejo Carpentier (writer).
José Lezama Lima (poet).
Nicolás Guillén (poet).

GLOSSARY

criollos	("kree-OH-yohs") Native-born Cubans, also known as Creoles.
El Jefe	("el EF-e") Literally, the chief. One of the more popular names by which Fidel Castro, Cuba's president, is known.
El tiempo especial	("el tee-EM-po es-spes-EE-ahl") The special period, a reference to the economic crisis presently afflicting the country.
Granma	The yacht that carried Fidel Castro, Che Guevara, and their followers to eastern Cuba in 1956, to overthrow the Batista government. The name *Granma* was adopted for Castro's organ of propaganda, the *Granma* newspaper.
machismo	("ma-KIS-mo") An attitude and a form of behavior that assumes male dominance.
orisha	("hor-ISH-ah") God or goddess in the Santería religion (see Santería, below).
peninsulares	("pay-nin-SOO-lah-rehs") Spanish-born Cubans.
Santería	("san-ter-RI-a") Chief Afro-Cuban religion practiced in Cuba.
Socialismo o Muerte	("soh-see-ial-IS-mo oh moo-AIR-teh") Literally, socialism or death. A political motto urging citizens to withstand the rigors of economic crisis.
son	("son") Indigenous music of Cuba.
Taíno	("TIE-noh") Early Indian inhabitants of Cuba, who arrived around A.D. 1200, but declined and became extinct in the 16th century after the arrival of the Spanish.
trova	("TRO-ba") A traditional ballad, once sung by traveling minstrels like the medieval troubadours.

BIBLIOGRAPHY

Nathan A. Haverstock: *Cuba in Pictures*, Lerner Publications, Minneapolis, 1987.

Edmund Lindop: *Cuba*, Franklin Watts, New York, 1980.

Emily Morris: *Cuba*, Heinemann Educational Books, Portsmouth, New Hampshire, 1990.

Victoria Ortiz: *The Land and People of Cuba*, J.B. Lippincott Company, New York, 1973.

Ana Maria Vazquez and Rosa Casas: *Enchantment of the World: Cuba*, Children's Press, Chicago, 1987.

INDEX

INDEX

INDEX